WITHDRAWN

THE SIXTIES IN AMERICA

The Sixties in America
History, Politics and Protest

M. J. HEALE

FITZROY DEARBORN PUBLISHERS
CHICAGO • LONDON

© M. J. Heale, 2001

Published in the United Kingdom by
Edinburgh University Press Ltd
22 George Square, Edinburgh

Published in the United States of America by
Fitzroy Dearborn Publishers
919 North Michigan Avenue
Chicago, Illinois 60611

Typeset in Monotype Fournier
by Bibliocraft, Dundee, and
printed and bound in Great Britain
by The Cromwell Press, Trowbridge

A Cataloging-in-Publication record for this book
is available from the Library of Congress

ISBN 1-57958-345-8 Fitzroy Dearborn

Contents

for Lesley

Introduction

No other decade of the twentieth century has acquired the mythological status of the 1960s. For the United States, this was the decade of the Camelot presidency of John Kennedy and the ruined presidency of Lyndon Johnson, of the great civil rights March on Washington and the assassination of Martin Luther King. It was the decade of the escalating war in Vietnam and the thrusting youth and peace movements, of urban riots and violent confrontations on the streets. These years also witnessed the birth of the New Left on the one hand and the angry conservatism of Barry Goldwater and George Wallace on the other, as well as a determined political activism that ranged from the atrocities of the Ku Klux Klan to the demonstrations of a revived women's movement. After the rather deferential politics that had characterised much of the 1950s, when traditional authority figures like President Dwight D. Eisenhower and FBI Director J. Edgar Hoover had commanded much respect, in the 1960s populist currents on both left and right threatened the command of established elites. It was a decade that saw the powerful eruption of rock music and the more tranquil dissemination of marijuana, and it ended with a walk on the moon.

Americans tend to remember – and sometimes revile – the Sixties as an essentially American phenomenon, but it was a decade that shook the world. It saw the Cultural Revolution in China, the Second Vatican Council in Rome, the death of the iconic Che Guevara in Bolivia, the massacre of students in Mexico, and barricades and near revolution in France. During 1967 the Beatles released *Sergeant Pepper's Lonely Hearts Club Band*, with its allusions to LSD in 'Lucy in the Sky with Diamonds', and Mick Jagger and Keith Richards of the Rolling Stones were given jail sentences for drug offences. Political and cultural influences readily crossed national boundaries in the 1960s, and student, feminist and other liberation movements around the world impacted on one another. The bipolar configurations of the Cold War world were coming under strain, as a schism emerged between China and the Soviet Union, as Czechoslovakia rebelled against Soviet control, as European imperialism continued its retreat, and as the formation of the European Economic Community created another potential centre of power. Nationalist and guerrilla wars in Asia, Africa and Latin America suggested to western radicals that the inspiration for revolution was to be found in the Third World. Some Americans framed their own struggles accordingly. The confrontation between black radicals and the white power structure in the United States could be seen as just a local example of a global phenomenon.

The American experience alone, however, has inspired a wealth of contentious scholarship. Countless accusations have been hurled against the personnel and movements of the Sixties. The biggest single target has been liberalism, because, by American definitions at least, liberals commanded the political institutions for the greater part of the decade. Liberals, notably those associated with the presidencies of John F. Kennedy and Lyndon B. Johnson, have been widely accused of failure, although the particular form of failure and the explanations for it have varied with the stance of the accuser. Radical critics have seen Sixties liberals as the creatures of corporate capitalism, more concerned to impede than to forward fundamental reform. Other scholars have argued that they were well-enough intentioned but that they bungled their policies and programmes. The Kennedy and Johnson administrations have been accused of raising expectations unrealistically and thus bringing on themselves the wrath of the militant left, as they have also been accused from a conservative perspective of pandering too readily to their favoured constituencies and fostering both dependency and permissiveness. They have been charged too with elitism, with engaging in arrogant schemes of social engineering, the impact of which they were not equipped to understand.

While those in and around government have been on the receiving end of most of the brickbats, charges have been levelled against others too. The New Left and the counter-culture have had their critics. Among other things, their members have been characterised as a 'destructive generation', as naïve, utopian and self-dramatising, indulging in fantasies that promoted violence and offered little of a constructive nature. Conservatives of the Sixties have not escaped either, for they have been charged with exploiting racism and with conducting repressive campaigns against their political opponents.

Many studies of the Sixties focus on discord, presenting a picture of a society 'coming apart' or 'unravelling', perhaps even close to anarchy.

'Suffice it to say that increasingly we will encounter one another as enemies', predicted American political scientist Andrew Hacker in 1970, anticipating one theme that would recur in subsequent analyses. But the Sixties and their actors have had their defenders too: liberals made mistakes but operated within severe constraints and nonetheless did something to improve the quality of American life, particularly for the poor and for minorities; the New Left may have nursed illusions, but also called authority to account and exerted a liberating influence; it would be claimed for conservatives that they had a better grasp of reality and human nature than their rivals and that they were right not to expect too much from government. The decade as a whole, its admirers have argued, bequeathed a more egalitarian political society and greater respect for a variety of cultural and lifestyle forms. The withdrawal of US troops from Vietnam and the forcing of both Lyndon Johnson and later Richard Nixon out of the White House have been cited as evidence that the political system 'worked'. Revolution was unnecessary and the social and political orders never near collapse.

The competing interpretations of the 1960s owe something to the continuing relevance of the decade, which still evokes strong emotions. Conservatives deplore Sixties values. In 1994 the right-wing Republican leader in Congress, Newt Gingrich, tried to turn the mid-term elections of that year into a referendum on what he regarded as the malign 'Great Society, counterculture, McGovernik' heritage of the 1960s, a strategy in keeping with his distaste for a president who seemed to personify the decade. Bill Clinton had come of age in the Sixties, during which he had shaken hands with President Kennedy, avoided military service and smoked pot, albeit without inhaling. The sex scandal which subsequently almost destroyed his presidency was also seen by conservatives as illustrative of the moral laxity he had presumably absorbed in his student days. The 'permissiveness' associated with the 1960s has been credited with the growth of drugs and crime, the 'break-up' of the family, and the rise of AIDS. Lyndon Johnson's War on Poverty, so the argument goes, has had the perverse effect of increasing dependency and triggering an enervating escalation of relief rolls. The foreign policy bungles of the Kennedy and Johnson administrations, especially the mortification in Vietnam, it has been said, destroyed American prestige in the world and weakened the capacity of future presidents to protect and further the US national interest. And an array of other ills has also been traced by various critics to the 1960s, such as an arrogant disregard for the Constitution as written by the Founding Fathers and the expulsion of God from American public life.

But for many the 1960s exercise a remarkable nostalgia. It was a time when 'right' and 'wrong' seemed clearly defined, when in particular there could be no doubt that the black and white supporters of the civil rights movement were on the side of the angels. In the eyes of some, the presidential administrations of the 1960s at least displayed a measure of sympathy for the weak and distressed, and tried to do something to improve the lives of disadvantaged people at home and abroad. It was a period when both governments and individuals seemed to be moved in part by more than self-interest, when it seemed easier than would later be the case to enlist in a cause. Modern civil libertarians pay homage to the decisions of the 1960s' Supreme Court, which pushed dramatically outwards the boundaries of the rights of the ordinary citizen. Liberation movements of all kinds – African American, women's, gay, grey – trace their origins to the 1960s. Some Americans credit the Sixties with releasing them from a Victorian moral code that they had found stifling. Students look with wonder and some envy at the extraordinary youth movement of the 1960s, at the demonstrations which seemed capable of humbling university administrations and even bringing down govern-ments. Many Americans of all ages exult at the explosion of rock music and the birth of the counter-culture, seeing the 1960s as a time when the obstacles to personal fulfilment were being swept aside.

While few scholars doubt that the Sixties were a tumultuous time, the precise parameters of the decade remain a matter for debate. Historical movements rarely display the tidiness of the calendar, and, as noted above, in the 1960s they also paid scant attention to national boundaries. The British historian Arthur Marwick, focusing on four western coun-tries, speaks of what he calls a 'long' 1960s, encompassing a cultural transformation which he dates from about 1958 and ending around 1974. American literary scholar Fredric Jameson, with an eye on the Third World, largely concurs, beginning his analysis with the late 1950s and locating an end 'in the general area of 1972–4'. John Morton Blum, a political historian of the United States, begins his study in 1961 and ends it in 1974, dates which respectively mark the presidential inauguration of John Kennedy and the resignation of Richard Nixon. Symbolic epi-sodes could be taken as markers. For the United States, the Sixties could begin in February 1960 with four black students sitting at a whites-only lunch counter in Greensboro, North Carolina, and demanding to be served, an incident that helped to spark the civil rights crusade, and end in May 1970 with the fatal shooting of four white students at a demonstration at Ohio's Kent State University. And if there is a case for a 'long' 1960s, it is also possible to argue for a 'short' 1960s, beginning perhaps with the celebrated March on Washington in August 1963, when Martin Luther King spoke movingly of his dream for America, and ending in 1968, when that dream was mocked by his assassination.

This is a study of the American experience, and since its focus is largely political the election of 1960 makes a convenient staring point. In that year, as it happens, both the right-wing group Young Americans for Freedom and the left-wing Students for a Democratic Society were organised, illustrations of the strengthening of the activist spirit, of the heightened visibility of young people, and of an emerging political polarisation. The United States did not lurch to the left in the 1960s, as is sometimes thought; rather middle-of-the-road politicians found themselves confronted by angry rebels at both ends of the political spectrum. One could also find other reasons for opening the Sixties in 1960, such as the authorisation for sale of the birth control pill, with its incalculable demographic and lifestyle implications. This study assumes that the Sixties came to an end in the early 1970s, although locating a precise date is difficult. The presidential election of 1972 has a strong claim, since while Richard Nixon's victory in 1968 had been a close one, in 1972 he won with a landslide, a decisive repudiation of the permissive Sixties values that had found their way into the platform of his opponent. Other dates also suggest themselves, such as 1971, when Nixon's panicky New Economic Policy exposed the serious weaknesses in the world's foremost economy, which could no longer sustain all the demands made on it, or 1973, when the United States signed a peace treaty with North Vietnam. The year 1973 also has other claims to attention, such as the Supreme Court's celebrated decision in *Roe v Wade*, which permitted abortion, another occurrence with unfathomable lifestyle implications.

A number of themes thread through the pages that follow. One argument is that the unusual activism of the 1960s can be seen not only on the streets but also in the White House and in the courts and even on occasion in Congress. It was a period that placed faith both in the potential of the individual and – for some years at least – in the potential of government. Government mattered to almost everyone. It was the extension of governmental authority that provoked much of the reaction on the conservative right, and it was the inadequacy of governmental action which intensified the radicalisation of many people on the left. Perhaps the most innovative organ of government was the Supreme Court, and the more suspicious right-wingers sometimes seemed to think that there was a kind of unholy alliance between the august justices on the bench and the unkempt demonstrators in the streets. This study also stresses the importance of economic and social forces and it risks slighting the significance of cultural change. Ultimately the counter-culture that emerged in the 1960s was to enjoy considerable success in penetrating the mainstream – even a Republican candidate for president in 2000 squirmed when asked about when he had last snorted coke. But the focus on Sixties culture in some recent accounts can obscure the fact that the economic and political systems themselves were changing in fundamental ways. The optimism and idealism which inspired so much of the activity of the decade rested in no small part on a buoyant economy, just as the darker and more introspective mood of the Seventies was related to the widespread realisation that a besieged economy could no longer perform miracles. Much the same could be said of the political system, which in the early Sixties offered itself as a vehicle of progress, but which in the aftermath of the decade has seemed incapable of supplying coherent and constructive government, at least at national level. Ultimately, of course, there is no neat demarcation between 'political' (or economic) and 'cultural' history, and this study discusses some of the ways in which these spheres impinged on one another. To many Sixties activists there was no distinction between art and life.

The contemporary ambivalence towards the Sixties is understandable, for the heritage of the decade was a mixed one. In some respects the United States reinforced its claims to respect as a democracy. Women, African Americans, Hispanics and others won greater recognition of their rights, and, in legal and political terms, a more egalitarian society was created. Government itself was made more accountable, as witnessed by the impeachment proceedings – almost unimaginable previously – brought against two presidents over the next generation. Even the recognition that there were limits to American power, both economic and military, can be regarded as constructive, painful though it was for some Americans to be stripped of the illusion of omnipotence. But it is difficult to view with equanimity other features that characterised American life in the last third of the twentieth century, such as the detachment from the electoral process of a substantial body of citizens and the astronomical gap separating the richest from the poorest Americans. The greater recognition that the Sixties gave to ethnic and cultural differences can be regarded as a positive accomplishment, although the identity politics of the late twentieth century sometimes seemed wearingly divisive.

A major argument here is that the Sixties formed a watershed, which is one reason why the decade evokes such powerful and contrasting sentiments. It separated one kind of America from another. Of course, since no society is ever held in suspended animation every period is an 'era of transition', but even so the 1960s stand out as one when seismic shifts took place. Briefly, the strains of the Sixties were related in part to the emergence of what is sometimes called a 'post-industrial' society.

At the crudest economic level, the decade was sandwiched between the bland 'affluent society' of the 1950s and the harrowing economic crises of the 1970s and the straitened circumstances of later decades. The old economy based primarily on the production of goods was giving way to an economy in which the provision of services took precedence, and advances in electronics and communications presaged the information age of the late twentieth century. A system of politics fashioned a generation earlier by a liberal Franklin Roosevelt finally disintegrated, and there emerged the first unanticipated signs of a seductive political conservatism, one which was to culminate in the election to the presidency of Ronald Reagan in 1980. It was a decade when the United States was bitterly humiliated in the jungles of Southeast Asia, when the vision generated by the Second World War that the 'American Century' had dawned was brutally punctured, bequeathing a lasting suspicion of the wisdom of the United States imposing its will in distant lands.

In these years too a respect for political leaders gave way to a popular distrust of government that would continue to constrain American administrations. A culture which cherished conservative conceptions of the family was increasingly undermined by the emergence of a variety of household forms, already becoming visible before the decade was over. Moral codes which owed something to Victorian notions of propriety were challenged by more relaxed attitudes and never regained their old authority. It was a decade that first witnessed those social and cultural forces which were to give rise to the 'culture wars' of the 1990s, displaying an apparently fragmented society at odds with itself, in contrast to the consensual sentiments that had seemed to be personified by the presidency of Dwight Eisenhower. In short, the 1960s were pivotal to the great transformation which American society underwent in the half-century after 1945. The strains associated with this transformation help to account for the turbulence of the decade, as the mutation itself goes a long way towards explaining the decade's schizoid reputation, for while some Americans welcomed the changes others were horrified by them.

PART I

Spirit and Context

Understanding the Sixties requires attention both to what was distinctive about the decade and to its location in a process of long-term change. What characterised public life was a pervasive activism, and this energy was grounded in part in the realisation that the country was being fundamentally transformed. In the Sixties it was widely assumed that the future should not be left to take care of itself. And broadly the outlook was optimistic. In a Gallup Poll of 1962, 55 per cent of respondents thought that 'life for people' would get better as opposed to 23 per cent who thought it would get worse.

The phrase 'the Sixties' tends to invoke images of marches and demonstrations, of student occupations and city riots. But street activity was only part of the story. A belief in the power of action penetrated almost every part of the culture, public and private. Individuals might act to fulfil themselves, groups might act to demand recognition, and courts and governments might act to promote the good society. Action, at almost any level, could make a difference. As such attitudes spread through the labyrinths of politics and culture they became mutually reinforcing, and were upheld by the received academic wisdom of the day, which tended to stress both the potential latent in each personality and the benign capacity of government. The activism of government and the activism on the streets went together, although some of the latter represented an attempt to build alternative institutions.

The activism of the era was in no small part a product of prosperity and of two decades of economic growth, which helped to generate the optimistic belief that anything was possible. (The buoyant economy also camouflaged growing economic problems that were not to be exposed until the end of the decade.) A changing economy also meant changing social and political systems, or the emergence of what is sometimes known as a post-industrial order. Among other things, post-industrial developments tended to enhance central bureaucracy, undermine the old class formations, erode the established party system, promote a managerialism which stimulated an adversarial reaction among the intellectual young, prise open opportunities for women and minorities, and allow cultural and lifestyle issues access to the social and political realms. Post-industrial theory, with its emphasis on the transformative powers of scientific knowledge, itself implied change, and necessarily called into question traditional forms. Such a basic reorientation of American life took time, and examining the Sixties means placing the decade in the context of a transition lasting the better part of half-a-century.

CHAPTER I

The Spirit of the Sixties: An Age of Activism

A striking feature of the 1960s was a pervasive belief in the power of action. Governments, groups and individuals, it was held, possessed the capacity to bring about change, and to bring about change for the better. Government could provide the conditions for economic growth, could protect the vulnerable, and could engage in a modest degree of social engineering to ensure that as many Americans as possible participated in the race of life. Groups could organise to protect and further their interests, to work for a better world, and to bring their concerns to the attention of courts and governments with some prospect of success. Civil rights organisations showed one way by popularising the techniques of direct action. Individuals too could act to fulfil their own dreams, to pursue their talents, even to 'find themselves' or to make themselves over. The itch for action was also expressed in the populist spirit which burst forth in the 1960s, whether in the form of the demand by left-wing students for 'participatory democracy' or in the grassroots protests that helped to buoy the campaigns of reactionary conservatives like George Wallace. Action was possible, it was widely believed, and produced results.

This spirit of activism helped to distance the era of the 1960s from the apparent placidity of the Eisenhower era. For many Dwight David Eisenhower, elected to the White House in 1952 and re-elected in 1956, had become the personification of the 1950s, a benign father figure who, it seemed, had presided but not led, who had sedulously avoided the 'bully pulpit' in favour of a management style that sought consensual solutions. At the time Eisenhower was criticised for spending too much time on the golf course, and when his term ended Gore Vidal observed that he had shown that the United States really did not need a president. Later scholars have been more generous towards him, though one of

11

the more positive assessments of the Eisenhower administration has characterised it as the 'Hidden-Hand Presidency', in which Eisenhower maintained a low public profile while actively managing the affairs of state from behind the scenes. Even this depiction, however, stresses the importance to Eisenhower of not being seen to take action.

In other respects too the society and culture of the 1950s had seemed to disavow excessive activism. Many American economists, particularly those on which government relied, still remained sceptical of Keynesianism, with its emphasis on a managed economy, instead harking back to the days of limited government, balanced budgets and a relatively unregulated market economy. This had also been the heyday of functional sociology, which in analysing society in terms of the respective functions of its various interconnected institutions, tended to assume that society was unchanging. 'The claim that functionalism cannot handle social change because it posits an integrated static society is true by definition', said the president of the American Sociological Association in 1959. The popularity of the psychiatrist's couch in the 1950s was related to the assumption that it was up to the individual to adjust to society; it was not the task of the individual to change society. Arthur Miller was distressed when his play, *Death of a Salesman*, was turned into a film in 1952, and the character Willy was depicted as a psycho, which, as Miller observed, 'melted the tension between a man and his society'. But in countless other ways too the political and cultural currents of the 1950s had seemed to militate against assertions of individual autonomy and social activism. The United States boasted more university and college students than any society in history, but these students were to become known as 'the silent generation'.

But by the turn of the decade a thirst for action was beginning to manifest itself, even among students, thousands of whom in May 1960 demonstrated in San Francisco against one of the instruments of orthodoxy, the House Un-American Activities Committee. The activism of the Sixties could find expression in many forms – in a confidence in the prescriptive powers of social scientists, in a benign view of the capacity of government to improve the common weal, in a belief that protest could be effective, in a conviction that the individual could find his or her inner self. In January 1960 the historian Arthur Schlesinger Jr predicted that 'the '60's will probably be spirited, articulate, inventive, incoherent, turbulent, with energy shooting off wildly in all directions'.

Schlesinger was not alone in identifying the American spirit with action and motion. Another historian whose ideas commanded respectful attention at the time was George W. Pierson, who in 1961 delivered an address entitled 'The M-Factor in American History'. The M-factor was mobility or movement, the defining feature of American history, in which the twin phenomena of immigration and the westward movement loomed large. Americans were a restless people, always in motion, and this was an aspect of their character as well as of their history. 'Movement means change', he said, for movement meant adaptation and exposure, so movement in all its forms turned Europeans into Americans, endowing them with a distinctive personality. Pierson was commenting on the American present as well as on the past. Jack Kennedy in 1960 campaigned with the slogan 'Let's get this country moving again'. When he was safely ensconced in the White House, the press gave some attention to the president's fondness for his rocking chair. Kennedy, it was said, liked to keep moving even when sitting still. (The president's critics might have been tempted to apply another definition of a rocking chair – it keeps you busy and gets you nowhere!)

As the urge to 'find oneself' suggests, the activism of the 1960s was closely related to a quest for autonomy. People, groups, governments, wanted to feel free to act, wanted however tenuously some sense of control over their own destinies. Here again an old American trait was asserting itself, the desire to be master of one's own fate, although in some 1960s formulations, and contradictorily, this could also imply some control of the fate of others. To say that activism characterised the 1960s is to say that people were seeking empowerment – the power of the individual, the group, the government.

A frustrating sense of powerlessness had emerged a little earlier in American culture. George F. Will has said that 'the 1950s were pregnant with the 1960s', and there were certainly signs of things to come as some Americans kicked against the constraints that bound them. Critiques of the conformity and blandness of American life had sometimes posited a solution in terms of a greater degree of individual authority. David Riesman and his sociological colleagues in *The Lonely Crowd* (1950) had defined 'other people' as the problem in a highly bureaucratised, crowded society, in which the individual rather passively followed the cues of others. This was the 'other-directed' personality that the authors believed that Americans were fast acquiring. But there was hope. Riesman and his co-authors saw 'at least the possibility of an organic development of autonomy'. They speculated that the very loneliness of the crowd would prove frustrating, and that 'people may, in what is left of their private lives, be nurturing newly critical and creative standards'. A flimsy variant of this attitude was found in William H. Whyte's *The Organisation Man* (1956), which suggested that the individual might resist organisational pressures and retain a measure of self-respect by cheating at personality tests! Daniel Bell in *The End of Ideology* (1960) spoke of the frustrating role of the intellectual in an age when the great ideological battles (as between collectivism and laissez-faire) seemed to be over, of the 'deep, desperate, almost pathetic anger' of young intellectuals in search of an elusive 'cause'.

This itch for expression was found elsewhere in the culture of the Fifties, not least in the writings of the Beat generation, with their emphasis on spontaneity and the pursuit of experience. A variant was expressed by Norman Mailer in 'The White Negro', in which he introduced 'the hipster', who understood that the only alternative to the deadening effects of conformity was to 'divorce oneself from society, ... to set out on that uncharted journey into the rebellious imperatives of the self'. Another kind of cultural rebellion was found in the eruption of Rock 'n' Roll, with the raw emotion and focus on authentic feeling of its lyrics. In J. D. Salinger's novel *The Catcher in the Rye* (1951), Holden Caulfield railed against 'phoniness' and James Dean in his filmic incarnations spoke for the angst of youth, in search of sincerity and meaning. A little later Betty Friedan opened fire against the gender conformity enjoined on women, their imprisonment in the 'comfortable concentration camp' of the home, and called on women to break out of the trap and find completion 'by fulfilling their own unique possibilities as separate human beings'. As with a man, she pointed out in 1963 in *The Feminine Mystique*, the 'only way for a woman ... to find herself, to know herself as a person, is by creative work of her own'. She seemed almost to be anticipating the title of Jerry Rubin's counter-cultural call to arms, *Do It!*

What helped to nudge this yen for action and expression into more vibrant life in the 1960s was a changing understanding of human psychology. Just as the number of middle class Americans flinging themselves onto the therapist's couch had been growing fast – the number of psychiatrists more than doubled in the 1950s – so had psychology and psychiatry become subjects of popular study. Americans were trying to understand themselves. The spread of Freudian psychology had served to focus attention on the personal rather than the environmental. More important, at least one major current in the science of psychology served to encourage the Sixties' assertion of self. What is known as humanistic psychology, associated with such figures as Abraham Maslow and Carl Rogers, was growing in influence in the profession. While drawing on selective strands of both psychoanalysis and behaviourism, humanistic psychology offered its own approach to the human condition, one which argued for the individual personality's capacity for conscious growth and change. As summarised by Ellen Herman, humanistic psychology emphasised among other things 'that the most urgent human needs were to feel good about oneself ... and grow emotionally; that "the self" was inherently healthy and contained a kind of divine spark that moved the human organism inexorably towards a process of growth and "becoming"; that "the self's" subjective experience was the highest authority ...'. Here was a psychology which looked not so much to the 'adjustment' of the individual to the larger society but to the liberation of the individual's potential. To promote such ideas, the *Journal of Humanistic Psychology* was founded in 1961 and the American Association for Humanistic Psychology in 1962.

Unlike some earlier psychology, humanistic psychology tended to send out an optimistic message about human nature and urged trust in 'the self'; the individual personality was capable of self-knowledge, transformation and fulfilment. The message was one of empowerment, of enhancing individual autonomy. 'I simply say with all my heart:' concluded Carl Rogers, 'Power to the emerging person and the revolution he carries within'. It was not much of a leap from that sentiment to the explanation of Black Panther leader Eldridge Cleaver: 'I had to find out who I am and who I want to be, what kind of man I should be, and what I could do to become the best of which I am capable'. Humanistic psychology helped to provide a rationale for the Sixties principle that 'the personal is political'. This was not a psychology that legitimated passivity. Insofar as the assumptions of humanistic psychology were absorbed by politically-aware youth in the 1960s, they reinforced optimism, encouraged a taste for action, and held out the hope of psychological liberation and therefore the liberation of society. 'We would replace power rooted in possession, privilege, or circumstance by power and uniqueness rooted in love, reflectiveness, reason, and creativity,' promised the New Left's celebrated Port Huron Statement.

It was sometimes said that psychology had replaced religion, although there were affinities between humanistic psychology and what was known as the New Theology as it emerged in the 1960s, one inspiration for which was the late German Protestant theologian, Dietrich Bonhoeffer. He had argued that human beings should act as if God did not exist, that is that they should not use him as a prop but should go out and search for him among the distressed. The New Theology promoted the view that humankind was responsible for its own predicament, that it had the capacity for action, and that it was up to individuals to bestir themselves to root out social injustice. The emphasis on the person was paralleled among Catholics in the Catholic Worker movement, which was also growing in the United States and which, with its suspicion of both communism and capitalism, offered individuals a path to pacifism and direct action among the poor.

If the New Theology helped to send men and women into the social movements of the 1960s, humanistic psychology's emphasis on the self had other counterparts in such fashionable religious phenomena as Eastern mysticism, hippie-style spiritualism, meditation, and Timothy Leary's drug-inspired League for Spiritual Discovery. Influential too, particularly among the college generation, were forms of existential philosophy. In the impersonal modern world, in this view, the individual could retain integrity, could give meaning to life, only by making choices or decisions. One was responsible for choosing, and personal action mattered. Engaging in protest activity could be seen as an example of the existential act, creating meaning through free choice and personal commitment, through an act of courage, whether or not the social or political objective was achieved.

The belief in the potential of the personality was paralleled in the early 1960s by a belief in the potential of government. Kennedy was excited by the untapped possibilities of the presidential office. The public, he said in 1960, 'demand a vigorous proponent of the national interest – not a passive broker for conflicting private interests'. On the eve of the election he quoted from Franklin Roosevelt: 'Better the occasional faults of a government living in the spirit of charity than the consistent omissions of a government frozen in the ice of its own indifference'. His successor had a yet bolder conception of the role of government. 'This administration believes in doing the greatest good for the greatest number of people', said Lyndon Johnson in explaining the War on Poverty. The liberal Democrats that peopled the administration for the greater part of the 1960s were no collectivists and had no wish to spawn a pervasive bureaucracy, but they did believe that government could make a difference. 'For a moment, it seemed as if the entire country, the whole spinning globe, rested, malleable and receptive, in our beneficent hands,' recalled Richard Goodwin of the early days of the Kennedy administration.

In part this faith in government rested on the relative success of the American economy during and since the Second World War, as it rested too on the recent remarkable advances in science, medicine and technology. In the early Sixties it was confidently believed that the major diseases could be conquered, and huge federal sums were devoted to causes like cancer research. The experts, it seemed, had the answers. The Second World War in particular illustrated the way in which a determined government could revitalise the economy, as it illustrated too the potential of technology. Further, in the war government had greatly increased funding for the social sciences, in the hope of securing a better understanding of human behaviour – and therefore of the means of shaping or manipulating it. The same need to mobilise the American people and resources and to understand the enemy continued to assure strong financial support for the social sciences through the Cold War. Federal monies for research in the social sciences multiplied five times between 1960 and 1967.

By 1960 there had been two decades of economic growth, and while Eisenhower's prudent economic management had its critics, the criticism was of the management, not of the economy itself. Sustained prosperity had vindicated American capitalism once again, even if its full potential was not being realized. Economists and other social scientists were claiming that they had the expertise to guide public policy, and their credibility was enhanced by the economic buoyancy of the early 1960s. The president of the American Economic Association observed in 1965 that 'economics is finally at the threshold of its golden age – nay, we already have one foot through the door'. In the following year the chairman of the president's Council of Economic Advisers agreed: 'Economics has come of age in the 1960s. Two Presidents have recognized and drawn on modern economics as a source of national strength and Presidential power. Their willingness to use, for the first time, the full range of modern economic tools underlies the unbroken US expansion since 1961'. The prospect of sustained economic growth into the future boosted optimism. And the United States was an 'affluent society'. The combination of abundant resources, sophisticated social scientists, and a well-directed government, it was widely held, should ensure that the country could at least solve its social problems. One group of economists and social scientists declared confidently in 1962 that the 'elimination of poverty is well within the means of Federal, state, and local governments'.

While there had been fairly steady economic growth for two decades, the incoming Kennedy administration fretted that there had not been enough, and indeed the Eisenhower years had been marked by occasional slowdowns. To the Keynesians around Kennedy such economic patchiness might be overcome by a more vigorous application of the 'new economics'. Eisenhower had been preoccupied with balancing the budget and had warned against repeated 'meddling' in the economy. To the impatient Kennedy men this meant that the potential of the economy was not being maximised, and armed with Keynesian tools they believed they could use the government's taxing and spending powers to 'fine tune' the economy and produce faster and more sustained growth. Further, faith in the new economics encouraged the view that an activist government could enter new territory. According to one of Lyndon Johnson's economists, poverty had hitherto been 'considered to be largely outside the proper realm of public policy', but that with the 'new economics' and the liberalism of the Kennedy and Johnson administrations, 'the view that solutions ... were the proper business of government gained currency and temporarily became dominant'. Within three days of becoming president, Lyndon Johnson remarked to his economic advisors that 'any problem could be solved'. Given the 'social need', exulted another member of the administration, 'the new knowledge can literally solve any problem'.

It was not simply social problems that could be solved. The optimism of the 1960s also rested on a confidence in the miraculous powers of science and technology. Since the 1940s penicillin and other wonder drugs had revolutionised medicine, the awesome potential of nuclear energy had been demonstrated, jet propulsion had been developed, electronic computers had been produced, and in ordinary households television sets had arrived and the versatility of plastic was enhancing the ingenuity of many consumer products. By the 1960s automation held out the prospect of replacing work with leisure. Federal spending on Research and Development increased six times in the 1960s, and the number of scientists and engineers employed in universities multiplied from 30,000 to 80,000. Faith in US technology underlay Kennedy's dramatic expansion of the missile programme and the launching of the moon mission. Even Adlai Stevenson, one of the more cautious members of the Kennedy and Johnson administrations, caught the bug, observing in 1965: 'Science and technology are making the problems of today irrelevant in the long run, because our economy can grow to meet each new charge placed upon it. . . . This is the basic miracle of modern technology. . . . It is a magic wand that gives us what we desire.'

'They literally swept into office, ready, moving, generating their style, their confidence – they were going to get America moving again. There was a sense that these were brilliant men, men of force, not cruel, not harsh, but men who acted rather than waited'. So wrote David Halberstam of the incoming Kennedy administration. These were men with good war records who saw themselves as 'hard-nosed realists', clear-minded and ambitious pragmatists who might be styled 'the best and brightest of a generation'. (Michael Harrington said of the student members of the New Left that 'they tend to be the brightest, the most restless and dynamic members of their generation'.) The very metaphor of the New Frontier carried this image of toughness and challenge, as it was also a call to action. 'It sums up not what I intend to offer the American people', said Kennedy, 'but what I intend to ask of them'. Personifying this 'can do' philosophy was the president's brother-in-law, Sargent Shriver. When asked in January 1961 to draft a plan for the establishment of a Peace Corps, Shriver submitted his report on a Friday morning in February and promised: 'If you decide to go ahead, we can be in business Monday morning'.

The Peace Corps itself early came to symbolise the Kennedy mission. It offered one response to the challenge thrown out by John Kennedy to his fellow Americans in his Inaugural Address: 'ask not what America will do for you – ask what you can do for your country'. The idea was to send American volunteers, mostly young ones equipped with educational, agricultural or health skills, into Third World countries to assist community development. In his election campaign Kennedy had promised 'a Peace Corps of young men and women who will be willing to spend two or three years of their lives as teachers and nurses, working in different countries . . . spreading the cause of freedom'. The inspiration for the Peace Corps was at once pragmatic and idealistic. It would serve the American cause in the Cold War, but would do so by displaying the better qualities of American civilisation.

It would illustrate the United States' willingness to hold out a helping hand to the 'peoples in the huts and villages of half the globe', of whom Kennedy spoke in his Inaugural Address. And it would provide an outlet for the idealism and energy of the younger generation. Here again were 'the best and brightest of a generation', or so it could be believed, for volunteers were rigorously selected.

If the Kennedy men took pride in their 'toughness', so did members of the Peace Corps. Applications from prospective volunteers poured in, some thirty or forty thousand a year in the early and mid-1960s. The greatest number of applications ever received occurred in the week following the assassination of John Kennedy. By the end of 1962 there were nearly three thousand volunteers in the field, and by 1966 some 15,556. A further benefit to the United States, argued Peace Corps champions, was that volunteers would return with their idealism tempered by knowledge and experience, that is they would make better citizens. When Sargent Shriver, anxious to convey the earthy reality encountered by many volunteers, offered a magazine an article entitled 'Failures in the Peace Corps', it was rejected on the grounds that the American public did not want to read about the Corps' weaknesses. As Shriver's successor as Director once put it, 'The Peace Corps is about love'. (Carl Oglesby, president of the radical youth group, Students for a Democratic Society, at about the same time also explained 'We want to create a world in which love is more possible'.) The Peace Corps was offering the world a definition of American identity and in so doing perhaps helped Americans to feel a little better about the national purpose. Kennedy hoped that the Peace Corps would counter Third World suspicions of the United States as an imperialist and militarist power with an image of an altruistic and idealistic America. If the programme did achieve any success in this respect, such gains were soon to be decisively reversed by the US role in Vietnam.

The 'can do' philosophy permeated the Kennedy and early Johnson administrations. 'Let's get this country moving again', Kennedy had repeated during his campaign. In fact, Kennedy was more interested in foreign than domestic issues, and he and his associates were impatient with what they regarded as the passivity of Eisenhower's handling of foreign affairs, which seemed to cede the initiative to the Soviet Union. His cherishing of the Green Berets and his interest in counter-insurgency represented one way in which the United States might help Third World countries resist communism. Lyndon Johnson was no less a 'can do' pragmatist with liberal ideals, though his primary interest was in domestic affairs. In 1964 Johnson asked Congress for a sweeping civil rights bill and a far-reaching tax cut, for an effective foreign aid programme and for legislation to 'build more homes, more schools, more libraries, and more hospitals than any single session of Congress' in American history. 'All this and more can and must be done', he asserted confidently: 'It can be done by this summer'. The belief in action, that there was a solution to all problems, inspired the extraordinary range of programmes that he launched under the banner of the Great Society. Johnson maintained an intense and continuing pressure on Congress to give him the legislation he wanted. 'Don't assume anything'; was how Johnson's Director of the Budget characterised the president's working style: 'make sure every possible weapon is brought to bear . . .; keep everybody involved; don't let them slacken'.

It was not merely the executive branch of government that displayed an activist will in the 1960s. Even more unprecedented was the extraordinary activism of the Supreme Court. The move away from the economic and welfare issues of New Deal politics towards issues relating to race, rights and lifestyle was partly the work of the judiciary. The Court had shown a greater willingness to exert its power of judicial review since Earl Warren had become Chief Justice in 1953, and the celebrated *Brown* decision of 1954, requiring an end to the teaching of black and white children in separate schools, was one mark of this. But by the 1960s the Court was straying into areas that had been all but unthinkable even at the time of *Brown*. In *Baker v Carr* (1962), for example, the Court asserted the right of the judiciary to strike down laws regulating election districts. This heralded the end of the power of states to manipulate election districts for partisan purposes, and, on the principle of 'one man one vote', the great majority of states quickly adopted reapportionment. The Court was reshaping the distribution of political power, usurping what many state politicians regarded as their prerogative to determine local voting regulations. The thrust of reapportionment was to afford greater political power to urban and suburban America; the Protestant hinterland lost some of its political influence.

Another fateful Supreme Court decision of 1962 ruled against the recital of prayer in schools, as an infringement of the constitutional separation of church and state. Cardinal Spellman of New York protested that the *Engel* decision struck 'at the very heart of the godly tradition in which America's children have for so long been raised'.

Conservative politicians of both major parties were enraged. 'For some years now the members of the Supreme Court have persisted in reading alien meanings into the constitution', fumed Senator Herman Talmadge of Georgia; '. . . they have sought in effect, to change our form of government. But never in the wildest of their excesses . . . have they gone as far as they did on yesterday'. The greater part of the influential metropolitan press came out against the Court. Even more stunning was the *Schempp* decision of May 1963 in which the Court ruled against the reading of the Bible and the Lord's Prayer in schools. Governor George Wallace of Alabama complained that 'we find the court ruling against God'. Some 150 resolutions were introduced into Congress calling for a constitutional amendment to allow prayers and Bible reading. The issue cut across party lines and seemed to present liberals as being 'against' and conservatives as being 'for' God.

If the Court seemed to be hostile to God it appeared to be friendly towards pornographers and criminals. The freedoms guaranteed to Americans by their Constitution underpinned a 1964 ruling that pornography could be prosecuted only if the material was 'utterly without redeeming social importance'. In *Griswold* in the following year the Court annulled a state law prohibiting the sale and use of contraceptive devices, in so doing developing the doctrine that there was a constitutional right to privacy. (The right to privacy had not been mentioned in the Constitution, but the Court decided that it had been 'implied', a decision that seemed to open the door to the infinite extension of constitutional rights.) In a series of decisions in 1963–5 the Court protected the rights of those accused in criminal prosecutions, obliging some states to release prisoners from their penitentiaries and hastily to revise their legal procedures. The celebrated *Miranda* decision of 1966 laid down standards for police questioning, making it clear that defendants from the outset had to be properly informed of their rights, including the right to a lawyer. Any confessions otherwise obtained would be invalid. The *Miranda* decision, which was decided by a 5–4 vote, revealed sharp disagreement within the Court itself. Justice Byron White complained that in 'some unknown number of cases the Court's rule will return a killer, a rapist or other criminal to the streets . . . to repeat his crime whenever it pleases him'. The decision met with howls of protest in Congress, and a public poll in November 1966 found that 65 per cent disapproved of the Supreme Court's position disallowing confessions obtained in the absence of counsel.

The Warren Court also seemed to be siding with demonstrators who chose to break the law. In Greenville, South Carolina, some black youths arrested while continuing a sit-in after the store had been closed had their convictions quashed in 1963, on the grounds that the state had been involved in an unconstitutional act of discrimination. In 1963 also the Court overturned the convictions of 187 African Americans who had been demonstrating in the grounds of the Capitol building of South Carolina. The Court rulings protecting sit-in and other demonstrators seemed to some to be an invitation to lawlessness. Even Justice Hugo Black, who had enjoyed a liberal reputation, complained in 1966 'that the crowd moved by noble ideals today can become the mob ruled by hate and passion and greed and violence tomorrow'. It is hardly any wonder that reactionary southerners were apt to detect communist conspirators behind both Supreme Court decisions and street demonstrations.

'We don't have a sick society, we have a sick Supreme Court', raged George Wallace during the 1968 campaign, describing as 'perverted' the decisions against school prayer and in favour of the distribution of 'obscene pornography'. The *Brown* decision of 1954 had made the Supreme Court a highly controversial and unpopular institution in the South, but by the mid-1960s public opinion generally was turning against the Court. When asked in November 1966 'How would you rate the job of the U.S. Supreme Court has been doing – excellent, pretty good, only fair or poor?', some 52 per cent of respondents opted for 'Only Fair-Poor' as against 48 per cent who thought the record 'Good-Excellent'. While the public broadly supported the Court's decisions on reapportionment and desegregation, it reacted strongly against the decisions disallowing confessions without counsel and outlawing school prayers.

The Court was not only protecting the New Frontier and Great Society legislation of the 1960s (in contrast to its attitude towards the New Deal in the mid-1930s), but was also forcefully expanding the area of individual rights. The strengthening of the constitutional rights of the individual meant also that national authority was growing at the expense of state and local governments. The Supreme Court reached over 200 decisions on criminal issues between 1961 and 1969, enmeshing local law enforcement officials in a host of constraints. The abuse of African Americans in particular at the hands of local officials was serving to undermine the traditional conception of federalism as a decentralised system.

In expanding individual rights the Court was introducing new and highly sensitive issues into the political world, especially criminal rights, school prayers, and pornography. Far from enforcing law, order and morality, as traditionally understood, the Court to some seemed to be encouraging crime and promiscuity. Civil libertarians were pleased by its decisions, and liberals were prompted to greater activism. But these new 'cultural' issues cut across the economic and welfare issues that had largely separated the major parties. In particular, they ate into the support for the Democratic party, which tended to be credited with encouraging such permissiveness. Many working and middle class whites who had embraced the New Deal were conservative on law and morality issues. 'They've put the Negroes in the schools,' complained one southern congressman, 'and now they've driven God out.'

The judicial activism of the Court was in part a response to the increase in the number of cases thrust upon it by protest activity. But its responsiveness in turn served to encourage further action. With the highest court in the land embracing libertarian and, so it seemed to many, permissive values, almost any kind of reform movement might hope for a successful result. Social reform and social protest were worthwhile in an environment in which the executive, legislative and judicial branches of government all seemed to be paying at least some heed. But as the Sixties wore on protest was also fuelled by the failure of government adequately to deliver on its promises. The activism of the Court and the 'can do' philosophies of the Democratic administrations had raised expectations, but these could not always be fulfilled. The liberal idealism which moved many public officials was itself in part responsible for the outbursts of dissent, and for the emerging distrust of hierarchies and of established institutions among many young Americans.

For many in the Sixties change would be and could be accomplished by 'the movement'. New life was breathed into the traditional American technique of the voluntary association. Perhaps not since the 1830s had there been such a faith in the power of the association, and specifically in the power of the association to act, whether for civil rights, peace, or feminism. Reform and protest movements proliferated in the 1960s, confident that action would bring change, a confidence which animated many established organisations as well as newer ones. The membership of the National Association for the Advancement of Colored People nearly doubled in the decade. But in a sense change was not always necessary. For many members of 'the movement' (any movement) what mattered was the existential act of commitment, the moral choice freely made, whatever the outcome.

The interlocking nature of the twin desires for self-fulfilment and social change were nowhere better exemplified than in the Students for a Democratic Society (SDS), which first emerged on the campuses in the early 1960s. Among the SDS's early targets were the impersonal nature of the large universities and the bureaucracy of modern life. In this reading, power had become overly centralised and the individual reduced to a cipher. To the SDS and other Sixties radicals, authority should flow upwards from the grassroots, not downwards from hierarchical structures, and they developed the idea of 'participatory democracy'. Whether in universities, businesses or government, it was held, individuals should have a voice in the decisions that affected them. It was the pressures arising from this stance that led to increased student participation on university committees. The SDS's Port Huron Statement spoke of the individual's 'unrealized potential for self-cultivation, self-direction, self-understanding', and the SDS held that the institutions of political democracy should be so designed as to give expression to this potential. Self-realisation was to be achieved through participation, though it was not easy to turn this organisational philosophy to the ends of specific social or political reforms. Trying to apply such theory to its own organisation, the SDS spurned formal leaders and engaged in endless and often unresolved debates. Action, in the form of participation, it seemed to many, was a good in itself.

Paralleling the political activism of the SDS and other New Left groups was the quest for personal expression pursued by participants in the counter-culture, which began to emerge in the mid-1960s. Smoking dope, revelling in rock music, and taking part in 'love-ins' afforded many young people an opportunity to achieve a measure of personal autonomy. But the counter-culture was also an instrument of change, or so some believed. Its disciples hoped that through disseminating their values among the wider population a fundamental transformation of society could be secured. The counter-culture found expression in art forms of all kinds – poetry, dance, theatre, film – and sought to communicate a spirit of insurgency and a new sensibility. A wholesale change of consciousness, some believed, could lead to peaceful revolution.

The emphasis on commitment, on self-expression, on 'finding oneself', so typical of the 1960s, could all too easily degenerate into a self-regarding narcissism, as it could also fall prey to the ingenuity of consumer capitalism. The 'Me Generation' of the 1970s were not so far removed from the flower children of the 1960s. The collapse of the New Left into the aggressive radicalism, posturing and mysticism at the end of the decade could almost have been predicted, once the impulse for individual autonomy took precedence over the desire for harmonious community.

By this date the Sixties' belief in action was in retreat. The formulae of economists and social scientists no longer seemed so compelling. The travail of the Great Society programmes cast doubts on the wisdom of projects of social engineering, while the agonising war in Vietnam simultaneously called into question the capacity of government to manage a complex world. 'The failure of liberalism', Daniel Bell observed, '... is, in part, a failure of knowledge'. Daniel Patrick Moynihan wrote in 1968: 'Somehow liberals have been unable to acquire from life what conservatives seem to be endowed with at birth, namely, a healthy scepticism of the powers of government agencies to do good'. He shortly joined the Nixon administration, where he suggested that the area of race relations might benefit from a period of 'benign neglect'. Experts, politicians and judges no longer commanded the confidence they had once enjoyed. Correspondingly, Americans held out less hope for the future. Only 39 per cent of those asked in a 1969 Gallup Poll thought that for people like themselves the world in ten years' time would be a 'better place to live in', while 55 per cent believed either that it would be no better or that it would be worse.

Not all activists lost faith in the value of protest activity, and the women's and environmental movements in particular continued to advance, while right-wing activists too took heart from the floundering of liberal reform. But with the disillusionment in the capacity of public policy to bring about a better world the power of organisation lost some its lustre. Some radicals abandoned the realm of politics and opted instead for the route of a purified personal consciousness.

CHAPTER 2

The Sixties in Perspective: Society, Economy and Polity

The grand visions nursed by American leaders in the two decades or so after 1945 for the better ordering both of their society and of the world were fuelled by an extraordinarily resourceful economy. The American economic juggernaut for a long moment seemed capable of fulfilling all the demands made on it. The prosperity of the 1960s made possible the War on Poverty, the mission to the moon, the frenetic arms race, the expansion of higher education, the well-heeled student revolt, and the war in Vietnam, as it also perversely encouraged the outbreak of rioting by the dispossessed in the cities. But the economy was not simply growing. It was also changing in exciting ways, or so it seemed to those who hailed the arrival of a new science-fired economy. Universities rather than factories were at the cutting edge of this new frontier. Further, economic growth was accompanied by far-reaching changes in the social and occupational structures. The proportion of industrial workers, for example, was declining, while the number of white-collar workers was rising fast, and the suburbs were growing in influence. A restructuring of the social order in turn carried implications for American politics, as old constituencies dwindled and others grew and as new demands were made on government.

Beguiled by a host of economic and social indices telling of accel- erating change, some analysts argued that the United States was moving from one kind of social structure to another. There were problems with the idea (associated especially with the sociologist Daniel Bell) that Americans were witnessing the emergence of a new 'post-industrial society', and others sought to develop alternative theories, but the thrust of this scholarship was that profound systemic changes were taking place. In Bell's formulation, for example, just as industrial society had supplanted agricultural society, so a post-industrial society

27

was displacing industrial society. In the heyday of industrialism the manufacturing sector had achieved pre-eminence, but now the service sector was displacing manufacturing as the lead element in the economy. White-collar workers had overtaken blue-collar in numbers, and those in professional and technical occupations were rising fast. Social and political values were meant to change too. In the 1960s, it has been calculated, seven out of ten net new jobs were created in the non-profit sector. With the growth of technocracy, of service occupations and of 'caring professions' like medicine, teaching and social work, an ethic of social responsibility might be projected. In these occupations people were less interested in making profits and more in enhancing the quality of life, and they might look to allies among a skilled managerial class. Social considerations might take priority in the making of public policy, and would be reflected in a greater degree of state planning, which would also be required by the increasingly complex economic system. Or so the post-industrial argument sometimes went.

Time has revealed weaknesses in this thesis. But such theories did underline the degree to which the 1960s functioned as a kind of pivot to the transformation of the American economic, social and political systems in the second half of the twentieth century. The American economy was already moving away from that made familiar by the industrial revolution. The America of heavy industry, of great battalions of blue-collar workers organised into industrial unions and arrayed against the forces of capital, was receding into the past. A new America, characterised less by class and more by greater occupational diversification, by cleaner working environments liberally sprinkled with white and pink collars, by science and technology and research universities, was rising up. A more differentiated order was being created, and its various organised segments competed for access to government. The passing of industrial society also meant the decline of the traditional work ethic, something which had long been happening but which also allowed for the increasing dominance of consumer culture. It allowed too for the stronger emergence of a hedonistic or self-expressive lifestyle, particularly among the young, which could be at odds with the rationalism of the technocrats. One implication of these complex changes was that political life might be less dominated by traditional economic and 'bread-and-butter' issues and be more receptive to lifestyle and cultural issues. Single issue groups, perhaps those devoted to civil rights or environmentalism, might secure greater visibility. Voter realignment might occur and the old party system be refashioned to reflect the new sociological contours. This indeed proved to be largely the case.

Statistics supported some of the observations about long-term change. If the old industrial economy is measured by the three broad areas of 'manufacturing', 'mining and construction' and 'transportation', these together accounted for a hefty 44 per cent of national income in 1950; by 1979 the figure was down to under 36 per cent. Conversely, the three service-oriented categories of 'finance, insurance and real estate', 'services' and 'government and government enterprises' together accounted for about 28 per cent of national income in 1950; by 1979 the figure was over 40 per cent. It was in the 1960s that the service sector overtook the industrial sector. The proportion of white-collar workers increased from 33 per cent in 1950 to 48 per cent in 1970 and to 57 per cent in 1990; conversely the proportion of blue-collar workers steadily declined, from nearly a half of all workers at mid-century to less than a third by its end. Farm workers were like blue-collar workers in that they produced goods too, but their numbers were also fast declining, dropping as a proportion of the workforce from about 11 per cent in 1950 to 4 per cent in 1970. The great armies of Americans who had previously produced goods – in foods or manufactures – were giving way to those who were being employed to offer services, whether in clinics, schools, banks, fast-food stores, real estate offices, or government agencies.

This extensive socioeconomic restructuring was accompanied – and in no small measure driven – by a considerable growth in science and technology, spurred by high defence spending and space projects. Since the Second World War national security and prestige considerations had meant an unprecedented governmental commitment to the expansion of education and science. In 1940 less than 1 per cent of the federal budget was spent on Research and Development (R & D); by 1965 the figure was 12.6 per cent, and the United States employed a higher proportion of scientists in R & D than any other country. In the 1960s computer systems came to be widely applied, presaging the astonishing growth of information technology of subsequent decades. Some technological innovations resulted from the billions poured into the space programme, and NASA (National Aeronautics and Space Administration) vividly symbolised the frontiers of science. In the thirty years after the Second World War, one in two Nobel prizes went to an American scientist; the proportion previously had been about one in seven.

Americans stayed in education longer, and the bigger universities became what one university president called 'multiversities', great factories of knowledge inculcating the skills needed by the workforce of a modern technological society. By the 1960s a tidal wave of post-war baby boomers was reaching these expanded universities, and some of these student millions proved restive with the technocratic values they encountered.

Yet many Americans were reassured by changes that seemed to afford a growing role to experts, to the technical and managerial classes. The number of professional and technical workers increased by 55 per cent in the 1960s, almost three times the overall rate of growth in employment, while the number of social workers doubled. In contrast, the number of machinists dropped by 25 per cent. Back in 1954, according to *Fortune* magazine, the typical middle-class consumer had been 'the machinist in Detroit'; ten years later the accountant or the computer programmer might have been cited. In fact, of course, service occupations included many low pay jobs, such as nurses and security guards, and the largest single occupational category by 1970 consisted of clerical workers. (Such categories kept up the size of the wage-earning class – by one analysis, some 57.5 per cent of working males were still working class in 1969.) These service workers tended also to be poorly unionised, union membership having suffered with the industrial economy. In 1955 over 33 per cent of the non-farm workforce were union members, but the figure slipped to 27 per cent by 1970. Twenty years later it was down to 16 per cent.

The changing socioeconomic structure (some argued as they contemplated such features as the diminishing proletariat) would mean a crumbling of the traditional class system. Education and training would be the key to social mobility, and the well-paid salary earners employed in corporate or government bureaucracies would not necessarily think of themselves as either owners of capital or as members of an industrial proletariat. The emphasis in post-industrial theory on the significance of an educated, white-collar workforce paralleled the arguments of some scholars about the emergence of a 'new class', one which was to inhabit the universities, the media and government bureaucracies, arguably exerting a disproportionate influence on the climate of opinion and public policy. When Richard Nixon was running for president in 1968 and again in 1972 he seemed to think, not without reason, that he was running against a 'liberal establishment' of this sort.

Changing residential patterns also pointed to the spread of a middle class lifestyle. Urban population continued to grow, but white-collar men and many blue-collar too, together with their families, were increasingly moving to the suburbs. Suburbanisation had been occurring for decades, but in the affluent post-war period it accelerated. In 1940 suburbanites had accounted for under a third of urban dwellers, but by 1980 were to reach 60 per cent, and it was in the 1960s that suburban population overtook that of the central cities. American politicians were soon paying more heed to suburban than to inner city voters. These voters were increasingly property-owners too; by 1960 over half of American families had become owners of their own homes. They were to constitute a formidable middle class. Conversely, African Americans were becoming increasingly concentrated in the big city centres.

Analysts were also beginning to note remarkable changes in the shape of society's most basic institution, the family itself. The post-war baby boom had peaked by the mid-1950s, when the birth rate had reached over 25 per thousand, and thereafter it had eased down, dropping more markedly from 1964. By 1968 the birth rate was only 17.4 per thousand, and the trend continued, slipping to 15.9 in 1980, below even the rather low rates of the Great Depression. There had been a trend towards marriage at a younger age in the 1950s, but this had gone into reverse by the 1960s, and a trend towards smaller families soon became apparent. The number of women having more than two children dropped markedly from the mid-1960s. If families were smaller, divorce was also changing their shape. Divorce rates, which had been relatively steady in the 1950s at around 2.5 per thousand, began to climb from the mid-1960s and reached 3.5 per thousand in 1970. By 1980 the figure was up to 5.2, capping yet another striking demographic trend that had its origin in the Sixties. The number of single-parent households also began to rise. The intertwining statistics were soon to provide evidence for politicians who perceived a 'crisis in the American family'.

Exactly how the declining birth rates and rising divorce rates of the 1960s were related to changes in the economic structure remains unclear, though similar demographic features were noted by other advancing industrial economies. The introduction of the contraceptive pill in 1960 helps to explain why married couples were having fewer children, as does the expense of keeping children in education until into their twenties. Divorce became more thinkable as women escaped the home to earn their own incomes, often in the expanding service sector, and the Sixties' emphasis on personal fulfilment encouraged many to put individual happiness above family commitment. But whatever the reasons for the reshaping of the family, it needs to be seen as part of the larger transformation of social life. And that in turn was in part related to the consumer values promoted by steady economic growth.

Since the 1940s the US economy had proved a remarkable success story, one that fuelled confidence in the capacity of government economists to deliver policies that would work. Gross National Product (GNP) increased by 250 per cent between 1945 and 1960. Occasional slowdowns triggered a few anxieties, but they were of short duration. The United States was an economic colossus, towering far above every other country in national income and productivity, and still accounting for about 40 per cent of world industrial production in the early 1960s, not much less than in the immediate post-war period. Further, the United States could claim some responsibility for the generally vibrant nature of the global and especially the western economy. A long export boom had produced a healthy trade surplus, which in turn meant that the United States could afford a massive capital outflow. Government aid and private investment abroad boosted foreign economies and pumped dollars vigorously around the arteries of the international monetary system. But the buoyant trade sector represented a relatively small part of the US economy, which was primarily sustained by high domestic spending. In contrast to the 1930s, American workers enjoyed virtually full employment, and their wages were rising too. Real wages increased by 50 per cent between 1945 and 1960, and a host of fringe benefits gave many workers a taste of middle-class lifestyles. The consumer society was reaching the masses.

The achievements of steady and sustained economic growth, plentiful job opportunities, and rising living standards for most American families suggested that the United States was getting something right. The American capitalist system seemed to be triumphantly vindicated. Further, the pervasive affluence suggested that government itself had more-or-less learned how to manage the economy, and the feel-good factor fostered expectations of even better times. Most people, it seemed, could look forward to rising incomes, to the possession of larger (perhaps suburban) homes, to ever more ingenious consumer products, to college education for their children and to more leisure for themselves. Americans could hope to fulfil the 'American Dream'.

Or at least, most Americans could. The pervasive prosperity cast into starker relief the plight of American minorities, particularly of African Americans. In 1960 about 60 per cent of them still lived in the South, where racial discrimination by law and custom remained strong. Most southern blacks were denied the vote and segregation was enforced in southern restaurants, parks, theatres and other public places. Even the school systems had made at best only token progress towards integration after the Supreme Court had declared segregated schooling unconstitutional in 1954. Southern blacks had long begun to vote with their feet, and their fast growing numbers in northern cities served to make northern politicians more receptive to demands for civil rights. Indeed, by 1960 blacks had become more urbanised than whites, some implications of which were soon to be revealed. But in the city ghettos too African Americans experienced inferior housing, educational and other facilities and discrimination in the labour market. Not surprisingly, the median income of non-white families nationally in 1960 was only about 55 per cent of that of whites, much the same as it had been ten years before. The blatant withholding of respect from African Americans angered them most deeply, but the affluence of white America, crudely flaunted by the popular culture and advertising of a consumer-oriented society, was an additional spur to the emerging civil rights movement. Many Hispanics too suffered from poverty and discrimination. But for many governmental officials the new economics had the answer to the poverty of blacks and others. A well-directed economy could benefit all Americans.

In the 1930s some of Franklin Roosevelt's advisors had wanted to promote the public good by a redistribution of income. By the postwar years most liberals had abandoned redistribution and instead put their trust in growth as a solution to economic and social problems. As John Kennedy said, 'a rising tide lifts all boats'. In this view, government should broadly be guided by Keynesian principles, accepting a general managerial role but limiting its direct intervention in the economy. In particular, economists had become sensitive to the need to promote consumer purchasing power as a means of sustaining growth. A number of labels have been applied to this economic philosophy, which characterised the Democratic regimes of the 1960s, such as 'growth liberalism' and 'commercial Keynesianism'. Kennedy's chief economic advisor described his policy as 'Keynes cum growth'.

Indeed, the American economy was to reach one of its highest points by the middle of the decade. Between 1961 and 1966 real output burgeoned by a third, and in 1965 growth reached over 6 per cent. But before the decade was out signs were surfacing that all was not well. Worker productivity began to level off. Very worrying was the emergence of inflation, which in the early 1960s had been under 1.5 per cent a year. But by 1966 inflation had crept up to 3 per cent and by 1969 had reached a disturbing 6 per cent. If these figures did not touch the astronomical heights of the following decade, they were enough to negate productivity and wage increases and they suggested that the American economy was becoming worryingly uncompetitive. Paralleling the emerging anxiety over economic performance was a growing concern over the damaging impact of industrial growth on the environment.

While most of the economic and social statistics spilling out of the expansive 1960s suggested a rosy future for the United States, they obscured certain long-term trends. Often overlooked was the degree to which the American economy was already subject to what would later be called 'globalisation'. Seen in a global perspective, the goods-producing economy in the second half of the twentieth century was not so much shrinking as being relocated, as the advanced industrial nations came to concentrate on white-collar tasks and left the dirtier jobs to the developing countries. US corporations themselves were contributing to an unfavourable balance of payments by the 1960s through capital investments abroad (much of it in Europe but increasingly in the Third World). In the 1960s alone the manufacturing capacity controlled by US companies abroad rose by over 500 per cent, far outdistancing the increase in domestic capacity. 'The world was our oyster,' fondly recalled one businessman. Funds invested in foreign plants were not being invested in domestic plant and machinery, a feature that contributed to the relative loss of efficiency by American industry. The level of government and private investment in the US economy was feeble by international standards. In 1960 it represented 17.6 per cent of GNP, compared to 30.2 per cent for Japan and 24.3 per cent for West Germany.

Given the low levels of savings and investments, it is hardly surprising that American productivity weakened. The United States, of course, started from a high point in 1945, when her economy was at full throttle while many other industrial nations were devastated, so that

American productivity increases were bound to be less spectacular than those achieved by the economies that were almost literally rising from the ashes. Nonetheless the average output per worker hour (in the non-farm business sector) generally improved by 2 to 3 per cent each year, healthy enough and faster than the inflation rate. The good times lasted for most of the 1960s, when productivity actually accelerated, but from 1967 the rate of increase slowed markedly. For much of the 1970s and 1980s the annual rate of growth in output per worker hour would often be less than 1 per cent, much less than the rate of inflation. One consequence was a decline in real family incomes, and the pinch was first noticed even before the economic turmoil of the 1970s. The real gross income of workers actually fell between 1968 and 1970. Suddenly the powerful engine of the affluent society was beginning to splutter. The changing economy, so welcomed by some Sixties sociologists, did not in fact herald good times for all. In the 1980s some scholars would use the bleak term 'deindustrialisation' to characterise the recent economic experiences of the United States, believing that it was seriously misleading to suggest that the economy had entered a new and improved 'post-industrial' phase.

The American position in the international economy, while a gigantic one, had been under threat for some years. The volume of US manufacturing output actually doubled in the quarter-century after 1950, but this was sluggish when compared to rival economies. France's manufacturing output multiplied nearly four times, Italy's by over five times, and Japan's by nearly twenty times. In 1950 the United States had produced nearly half of the world's steel; by 1970 the share had slipped to about a fifth, and the decline was to continue. 'The rest of the industrialized free world has been narrowing the economic gap with the U.S. at an outstanding rate,' noted an article in *Fortune* in 1967. As the industrial capacities of other countries soared, some of their products found their way to the United States. The country's extraordinary industrial strength had meant that since 1893 there had been a trade surplus every year. This surplus in fact survived the 1960s, but during the decade imports were rising faster than exports, and by 1969 the favourable balance on trade in merchandise, which had reached $6,801 million in 1964, had shrivelled to less than a tenth of that. The account was finally to slip into the red in 1971, and it remained that way in most years for the rest of the century. In 1960 foreign automobiles had barely begun to penetrate the US, with their share at 4 per cent; by 1970 it was

17 per cent and the proportion continued to rise relentlessly. In other areas too American manufacturers found their domestic markets invaded by foreign goods.

What made the loss of the trade surplus serious was the fact that the United States had been running deficits on other international accounts, because of military and other commitments abroad, so that her overall balance-of-payments had long been negative. Crisis struck in March 1968, when there occurred what *Time* magazine called 'the largest gold rush in history'. The immediate problem was the payments deficit. Since the Bretton Woods Agreement of 1944, the United States had effectively operated as the world's banker, with the dollar serving as a reserve currency. Dollars could be converted to gold on the request of foreign central banks. A modest balance-of-payments deficit could be tolerated, but from the mid-1960s the deficit was rising, as was inflation. Sterling was also under pressure, and the British government devalued the pound in December 1967, precipitating a frenzied selling of currency for gold in the money markets. For the moment international bankers managed to hold the price of gold, but (after US reverses in Vietnam) the run on the dollar resumed in March and vast quantities of gold disappeared from the reserves. The United States hastily patched up the Bretton Woods system and again saw off the speculators, but the relief was short-lived. The balance-of-payments was soon deteriorating once more. In 1971 ferocious speculation against the dollar resumed, and in August President Nixon temporarily suspended the dollar's convertibility into gold; he finally abandoned it in 1973. Dollars could no longer be changed into gold, the United States was retreating from the role of world banker, and Bretton Woods was dead. The dollar remained a major currency, but floating exchange rates henceforth would characterise the international monetary system. The dollar's domination was over.

The humbling of the dollar closely coincided with the American humiliation in Vietnam, and the two were connected. The war had fuelled rising inflation and had diverted resources from innovative investment that might have made industry more competitive. Americans were discovering that US power had its limits. Economic strains and foreign policy reverses were also to have a profound impact on the way Americans conducted their politics. Like the economic system, the American polity was also being transformed. One fatality was the New Deal Order, a term sometimes applied to the heritage of Franklin

Roosevelt. This implied a rightward shift in American politics, but the public's distrust of politicians also grew and coherent government of any political persuasion was to become more difficult to achieve.

At the optimistic advent of the Sixties most Americans were agreed on the main principles of government policy. Leading members of the Democratic and Republican parties adhered to what has been called 'consensus liberalism' or alternatively 'the vital center', that is an acceptance of a modest welfare state at home and commitment to the containment of the Communist bloc abroad. It was also a way of viewing politics that had tended to place faith in federal (as opposed to state or local) authority. But this consensus proved a fragile one and it did not survive the decade. Mainstream politicians were shaken by revolts from both right and left, and at both ends of the spectrum there were grassroots resentments directed at Washington.

The Democratic party had been the majority party since 1932, when Franklin Roosevelt had been swept into the White House, and its majority status had been sustained by what may be called the New Deal Order. The New Deal itself, as a series of economic and social reform measures, had lasted only from 1933 to 1938, but the larger New Deal system of politics survived into the 1960s. Through these decades the Democratic party broadly identified itself with a liberal agenda, if liberalism is defined in its modern American sense as a faith in the benign capacity of government, a sympathy for a modest welfare state, and some sensitivity to labour and ethnic constituencies. Further, most Republican leaders accepted the structures that Franklin Roosevelt had created. This is not to suggest that Congress was kept busy with liberal legislation, for its conservative bloc was generally able to frustrate reform proposals. But the potential for reform remained. When President John F. Kennedy was assassinated and public opinion rallied behind his programme, and when Lyndon Johnson's election to the presidency in 1964 was accompanied by landslide victories in Congress, the conservative bloc was overwhelmed. The mid-1960s witnessed a whirlwind of reform legislation.

The ascendancy of the Democratic party in the middle third of the twentieth century arose from the voter realignments of the 1930s, as the urban working and middle classes and African Americans in the North lined up more firmly behind it. It rested also on the longevity of the New Deal coalition. This loose alliance of voting groups remained in existence to elect John Kennedy to the presidency in 1960 and Lyndon

Johnson in 1964. The Solid South (where the Democrats had tradition-ally been virtually the only party and where most blacks could not vote), the big city machines, the industrial unions, urban white 'ethnics' (such as Polish and Italian Americans whose families had arrived with earlier generations of European immigrants) and African Americans uneasily cohered to give the Democratic party its majorities. It also gave the Democratic party its split personality, for in the post-war period its southern wing became increasingly conservative as its northern elements proved sympathetic to civil rights. Consensus liberalism was dependent on the survival of the New Deal coalition, and that in turn rested on a capacity to turn a blind eye to the condition of southern blacks.

The personal popularity of Dwight Eisenhower had enabled the Republican party to win the presidential elections of the 1950s, but in 1960 Democratic hegemony was restored, albeit narrowly. The youth-ful John F. Kennedy projected an image of vigour, identified himself with a rather mild New Deal liberalism, and above all promised action. His Republican opponent, Richard Nixon, also offered economic growth at home and the containment of communism abroad, but Kennedy won the day. With a lead of only 0.17 per cent in the popular vote Kennedy could hardly claim a mandate, and the Democratic majorities in Congress were trimmed as well. But the New Deal coalition had restored Democratic ascendancy in both the executive and legislative branches of government.

The New Deal coalition achieved its last great national victory in 1964, with the election of Lyndon Johnson to the presidency by a landslide. Within the Democratic party Johnson faced a revolt led by George Wallace, the segregationist governor of Alabama, who entered the primary elections mouthing a crudely-concealed racism. Johnson saw off this insurgency, but not before Wallace had unnervingly won about a third of the primary votes in the northern states of Wisconsin and Indiana. Not all Democratic voters, it seemed, were happy with the domestic policies of the Johnson administration. The Republican party also experienced a revolt against 'consensus liberalism'. In a carefully organised campaign, buoyed by a grassroots activism, the right-wing Senator Barry Goldwater of Arizona wrested the leadership of the party from the 'Me Too' Republicans that he believed had been meekly following the Democratic party line.

The 1964 election cannot be regarded simply as a referendum on New Deal/Great Society reform, since the issue of Vietnam loomed large, but Goldwater clearly targeted traditional liberalism. He railed against the 'cancerous growth' of governmental bureaucracy, called for a 25 per cent tax cut and talked about making Social Security voluntary. He travelled to impoverished West Virginia to assail the Great Society's 'phony war on poverty', to Tennessee to attack the New Deal's celebrated Tennessee Valley Authority, to the farm states to criticise agricultural subsidies, and before the elderly citizens of Florida he denounced 'the outright hoax of this administration's medicare scheme'. Goldwater had also voted against the Kennedy-Johnson civil rights bill in the Senate. The Democrats suggested that the 'trigger-happy' Goldwater would precipitate a nuclear war if elected. Lyndon Johnson for his part never lost an opportunity to cloak himself in Franklin Roosevelt's mantle. His acceptance speech at the Democratic convention was modelled on Roosevelt's of 1932, and in the campaign he cited Roosevelt as the man who 'electrified a nation, and ... saved a republic'. He ended one speech with a famous Roosevelt phrase: 'The only thing that America has to fear is fear itself'. One working man summed up his reaction to the campaign: 'Everything I got, I got under a Democratic administration. You name it – unemployment compensation, Social Security. Goldwater seems to want to tear down a lot of these laws that were made 25 years ago'.

Lyndon Johnson won in a landslide, securing 61 per cent of the popular vote and forty-four of the fifty states. His coat-tails also increased Democratic majorities in both houses of Congress. Many elements of the New Deal coalition contributed to the victory. Organised labour had enthusiastically rallied to Johnson, spending huge sums on the party's behalf and conducting fierce registration drives. Low income voters generally were overwhelmingly for Johnson, as were Catholics. Some 90 per cent of Jewish voters went for Johnson and an extraordinary 94 per cent of African American voters, with whom Johnson was proving even more popular than Franklin Roosevelt. The big city states were loyally and strongly for Johnson, the surviving urban machines like Mayor Richard Daley's in Chicago performing their time-honoured role. And Johnson carried much of the traditionally Democratic South.

But stunning though the size of the victory was, there were signs of cracks in the imposing New Deal edifice. Most obviously, Goldwater had carried five states in the Deep South, which also broke with its own past by returning a handful of Republican congressmen. The

Democratic administration's record on civil rights had alienated many of its erstwhile southern supporters. Goldwater had shown Republicans that the banner of a racially-tinged conservatism could break the Democratic majority. There were also ominous flickers of dissatisfaction with the old New Deal coalition elsewhere. Among some Irish and Italian Catholic wards in New York City Goldwater improved on Nixon's 1960 showing, as he did also in Polish Catholic wards in the industrial Midwest. Earlier in the year, the surprisingly large votes secured by George Wallace in the Wisconsin, Indiana and Maryland primaries had also heavily hinted at the strains in the Democratic coalition. In the past populist or grassroots politics had normally been associated with the left; in the 1960s a right-wing populism was emerging.

By 1966 the signs of a 'backlash' against Great Society policies were stronger. The ghetto riots which had erupted in 1964 proved not to be a passing phenomenon; there were even bloodier outbreaks in 1965 and 1966. The apparent crumbling of law and order distressed Americans of all races, while some white citizens cooled towards programmes designed to give benefits to African Americans. As the Democratic governor of California put it: 'Whether we like it or not, the people want separation of the races'. In June 1966 one columnist observed of Great Society reform that 'the alliance of labor, Negroes, middle-class white liberals, and machine politicians upon which that strength was based is coming apart'. The Republicans did well in the 1966 mid-term elections, winning two-thirds of the races for state governor. The huge majorities that Johnson had helped to produce in his 1964 landslide in both houses of Congress were cut back, from 155 to 60 in the house and from 36 to 28 in the senate.

Just four years after its 1964 triumph the Democratic party was tearing itself apart. In 1964 the principal opposition to Johnson's consensus politics had come from the strident Wallace and Goldwater elements on the right, but by 1968 the New Left had become a significant political force and was questioning the legitimacy of his administration and particularly of its foreign policy. The disastrous course of the war in Vietnam, the unprecedented anti-war demonstrations, and the continued explosions of violence in the cities together created an image of a society that was coming apart. Johnson faced revolt from within his own party, as first liberal (and anti-war) Senator Eugene McCarthy of Minnesota declared himself a candidate for the

Democratic presidential nomination, and his strong showing in the New Hampshire primary in turn encouraged Senator Robert Kennedy of New York to enter the contest. The beleaguered president, his personal standing in the polls hitting a new low, announced on 31 March that he would not be a candidate for re-election.

The Democratic party was being pulled in three different directions. On the left were anti-war Democrats, mostly liberals and some close to the campus New Left, who wanted to get the United States out of Vietnam and to extend the social reform agenda. In the centre were those who remained loyal to the Johnson administration, whose new champion was to be the vice-president, Hubert Humphrey. On the right were those who had had enough of the Great Society and who seemed to hanker for a strong hand to smite the Communists abroad and to discipline the rioters and unruly students at home. By 1968 this tendency seemed to be on its way out of the party. In 1967 George Wallace had founded the American Independent party in order to run as a third-party candidate for president, and he hoped to recruit 'white backlash' voters to his cause. Richard Nixon too, as the presidential candidate of the Republican party, would also be targeting these voters. Both Wallace and Nixon embraced the cause of 'law and order', which in the aftermath of the ghetto riots carried a racist echo.

The presidential wing of the Democratic party was badly hurt by the disturbances surrounding the national convention in Chicago in August (by which date Robert Kennedy was dead). Anti-war demonstrators staged raucous protests outside the convention hall, and inside the Johnson forces ruthlessly pushed through Hubert Humphrey's nomination. Tied to the unhappy Johnson presidency, Humphrey found it difficult to mount an effective campaign. Richard Nixon won the election with 43.4 per cent of the popular vote, just topping Humphrey's humiliating 42.7 per cent. George Wallace fared remarkably well for a third-party candidate with 13.5 per cent of the vote, and he carried five southern states. Since Johnson had achieved over 61 per cent of the popular vote only four years earlier, this outcome represented a colossal reversal for the Democrats. Twelve million 'Democratic votes', as it were, had gone missing. The party of reform had been repudiated, as the majority of voters opted for the two varieties of conservatism. Gallup polls sent a similar message: between 1963 and 1969 the proportion of respondents identifying themselves as 'liberal' dropped from 49 to 33 per cent.

The South's long identification with the Democratic party was finally over. Apart from Lyndon Johnson's Texas and the border states of West Virginia and Maryland, the South had gone for Nixon or Wallace. Nixon remarkably secured a margin of half-a-million votes over Humphrey in the once 'solid' South. Democratic presidential candidates could never again count on the section to deliver them a substantial bloc of electoral votes. And the Democratic orientation of urban working and middle class ethnics in the North continued to weaken. Union leaders reported difficulty in dissuading members from defecting to Wallace, and 9 per cent of northern manual workers indeed voted for him. As political analysts Richard Scammon and Ben Wattenberg observed, in 1968 the New Deal coalition was 'shaken loose from its moorings'. The Republican task in the 1970s, they concluded, was 'to shake loose more of this vote and to see to it that more of it goes to the Republican side'.

Broadly speaking, the centre of gravity in American politics had moved to the right, although the shift was a little uncertain. The Democrats retained control of both houses of Congress, albeit with reduced majorities. (For the first time since 1848 a president was returned to the White House without his party winning control of either house of Congress.) The rightward thrust continued. It had been George Wallace who had demonstrated how the New Deal coalition might be destroyed, and no-one absorbed the lesson better than Richard Nixon. The populist Wallace had presented himself as the champion of an embattled white working-class resisting the social engineering programmes of bureaucratic and Democratic elites. Nixon might hope to fashion a 'new Republican majority' by carefully positioning himself on civil rights issues, never openly racist but speaking to the growing anxieties of white Americans in both North and South. Strategist Kevin Phillips argued in 1970 in *The Emerging Republican Majority* that the Nixon and Wallace votes together could be the basis for a new Republican ascendancy, augmented by demographic processes which were strengthening the political clout of the 'Sunbelt' stretching across the western and southern states.

As Nixon searched for a formula which would convert his slim win in 1968 into a permanent Republican majority, the Democrats compulsively came to his aid. The charged scenes at their Chicago convention had discredited the moderate leadership and allowed a political advantage to the left, which overhauled the party's nominating process in accordance with the principle of 'maximisation of participation', resulting in the widespread use of primary elections and improved access for women and racial minorities. The 1972 presidential convention was quite unlike any before it. Women had constituted 13 per cent of delegates in 1968; in 1972 they were 40 per cent, while the proportion of delegates aged under 30 soared from 3 to 22 per cent, some of them veterans of the New Left. Even more extraordinary, Mayor Daley's Chicago delegation, including Daley himself, was excluded because it had apparently not respected the new rules. One journalist, noting the paucity of Italian and Polish names among the democratised Chicago delegation that was seated, observed: 'Anybody who would reform Chicago's Democratic Party by dropping the white ethnic would probably begin a diet by shooting himself in the stomach'. The mayors of several large cities, including Detroit, Boston, and San Francisco, were also absent. But the better representation of certain 'minorities' was bizarrely achieved at the cost of skewing the party's class base. The new delegates often had high-income jobs. The rise of white-collar activists within the Democratic party did not mean that the party was pulled to the right; rather the reverse, at least for the moment. Many advocated a broad reform agenda, but one that focused less on economic and blue-collar issues after the fashion of the New Deal and more on lifestyle and rights issues. Some young long-haired delegates were touched by the counter-culture, urging the legalisation of marijuana and recognition of gay rights. The 1972 platform called for an 'equitable distribution of wealth and power', improved welfare rights, school bussing, the recognition of the 'constitutional and human rights' of prisoners, and even 'the right to be different'. George McGovern, who favoured getting out of Vietnam and extending amnesty to draft-dodgers, won the nomination, but his campaign was to be fatally associated with the three As: 'acid, amnesty, and abortion'.

Richard Nixon, wooing Independents and conservative Democrats, won the 1972 election with 60 per cent of the popular vote and carried forty-nine of the fifty states. The New Deal coalition was now in ruins. Nearly 40 per cent of those who usually voted Democrat cast their ballots for Nixon, who became the first Republican candidate to win a majority of Catholic voters. With Wallace out of the picture Nixon swept the South, taking over 70 per cent of the popular vote there. Of the traditional New Deal constituencies, only African Americans and Jews remained strongly in the Democratic column in the presidential election.

But neither in 1968 nor in 1972 was Richard Nixon able to translate his electoral appeal into Republican majorities in Congress. The 'new Republican majority' never materialised, not at any rate in the form of a political force that could simultaneously win majorities at all levels of American politics. The phenomenon of split-ticket voting was growing, as Americans voted one way in presidential and another way in other elections, and from the Nixon administration onwards the party occupying the White House has generally faced majorities of the other party in Congress. In place of the New Deal Order, a divided political authority characterised American politics in the last third of the twentieth century. For most of those years, and beginning in 1969, a Republican president found himself poised against a Democratic Congress.

The destruction of Democratic hegemony was in part a product of the erosion of the regular party system. The party machines had been weakening for years, as television allowed them to be circumvented and as suburbanisation put voters beyond their reach, and voter turnout at elections had been dropping. A post-war high had been reached in the presidential election of 1960, when 62.6 per cent of the potential electorate had turned out. In 1968 turnout slipped to 60.9 per cent, and it was down to the mid-50s in the presidential elections of the 1970s. (In many western European countries turnouts of over 70 or even 80 per cent are quite common.) In non-presidential elections turnout was even lower, with perhaps only a quarter of the voting age population going to the polls. Walter Dean Burnham has remarked that 'the shift toward voting abstention since 1960 is by far the largest mass movement of our time'. The turnout of manual workers in particular seems to have dropped markedly between the 1960s and 1980 (reflecting in part the decline of union members in the economy). In brief, constituencies that in the past were usually Democratic saw an erosion in their degree of electoral participation. The party machines and labour unions were no longer able fully to mobilise them.

The post-1968 reforms of the Democratic party accentuated this process, as candidates looked to special interests and middle-class activists for financial and organisational support. While the radical fringe that gave the party its extremist air in 1972 was shaken off, the Democrats who thereafter came to the fore were not the New Dealers of old. The trend towards the use of primaries continued, in which low turnouts gave a disproportionate influence to the voting middle classes. Increasingly Democratic politicos were recognising the importance of the middle classes and of the suburbs, and while liberal on many social issues (such as abortion) tended towards more moderate positions on economic and welfare measures.

The weakening in party organisation was also reflected in a decline in partisanship. In the heyday of the New Deal Order most voters voted the straight party line in all elections. In 1960 only 14 per cent of voters voted for different parties in presidential and congressional elections, and the figure was barely higher in 1964. But in 1968 it suddenly jumped to 26 per cent, and it was to remain high (settling at around 25 per cent). There was other evidence too that voters were becoming less partisan. In 1960 some 75 per cent of electors identified themselves as either Republicans or Democrats; 23 per cent called themselves Independent. Again it was in the second half of the 1960s that the per centage of those describing themselves as Independent began to climb sharply, to 29 per cent in 1968 and to 35 per cent in 1972, by which time the proportion identifying with the two major parties had dropped to 63 per cent. Thereafter, for the next two decades, the proportions remained much the same. During the few years on either side of 1970 something was happening to tear large numbers of voters away from their traditional allegiances. The strong partisanship which had characterised the New Deal Order, and indeed earlier models of American politics, did not survive the 1960s intact.

If the Democratic party was not the mighty organisation that it had been, the Republican party began to display rather more vigour. Some of the voters won over from the Democrats during the elections of 1968 and 1972 remained with it. The Republicans also felt obliged to follow the Democrats in democratising their procedures and relied more on primary elections to select members of presidential conventions, allowing populist pressures greater access. While the fortunes of the Republican party did not revive sufficiently to give it a secure majority status, its activists imparted a new energy even as they nudged it to the right. And the party was buoyed by the conservative direction being taken by a range of political, economic and religious ideas.

By the end of the 1960s some intellectuals were moving away from the big government ideas associated with New Deal reformism. The apparent failure of the Great Society to deliver on its promises, together with the rising inflation and slowing economic growth, was casting doubt on the capacity of government to manage a complex society. These intellectuals, many of them Democrats, were later to become known as 'neoconservatives'. While many insisted that they remained liberals, they stood against the New Leftist and counter-cultural fringes of the Democratic party, questioned the degree of social engineering in Great Society programmes, and upheld traditional family and cultural values. Neoconservatives were also keen to maintain a clearly anti-communist foreign policy. A few joined the Nixon administration, such as the blunt-speaking Democrat Daniel Patrick Moynihan. Their well-publicised ideas eased the emergence of a more conservative style of politics.

The disconcerting trends that emerged in several economic indices in the late 1960s grew more ominous in the 1970s, strengthening the reaction against Keynesian and 'big government' solutions. The Chicago economist Milton Friedman won a wide audience for his free market and monetarist ideas, and the Republicans benefited from this new respectability of conservative economics, doctrines which for the most part limited government action. But strengthening the Republican cause too was a new cultural and religious conservatism. By the mid-1970s an informal collection of conservative interests known as the New Right was coalescing, energised in part by antipathy to the New Left and Sixties counter-culture. What distinguished it from older forms of conservatism was its emphasis on a range of social, cultural and moral issues. New Right activists were generally hostile to abortion, women's and gay rights, court-ordered bussing and bans on school prayers, and to permissive attitudes regarding sexual morality and personal freedom. Nonetheless they shared with other conservatives a preference for free market economics. The New Right also benefited from a strong growth in evangelical and fundamentalist Protestantism.

The renewed energy of the Republican party thus owed much to reactions against the big government economic policies and the 'permissive' social policies and Supreme Court decisions of the 1960s. These currents were eventually to help carry Ronald Reagan into the White House in 1980. But the Republican party had also been moved to the right, which served to limit its appeal, and it found it easier to win presidential elections than to gain control of Congress. The New Deal Order was replaced not by a Republican ascendancy but by divided government.

The economic and welfare issues that had separated the two major parties during the years of the New Deal Order had not vanished but other issues had emerged to cut across these traditional lines, producing a fissured style of politics. The Democratic party retained within it many still holding to a New Deal philosophy, but they mingled uneasily with a new breed of Democrats who were cautious on economic and welfare issues though usually liberal on race. Big business and the very rich remained most comfortable with the Republican party, but that party also contained people who were unhappy with the sometimes illiberal attitudes of fellow members on race, abortion and lifestyle. Democratic hegemony had foundered on issues related to race, culture and foreign policy, which diverted to the Republican banner some Americans who otherwise preferred Democratic economic policies.

This confused system of politics had its origins in the turbulent days of the 1960s, when personal and foreign policy issues had erupted into the political arena and when far-reaching socioeconomic change had chipped away at the foundations of the New Deal Order. Many of the processes associated with the emergence of a post-industrial society, with its redistribution of occupational prestige, its weakening of traditional class ties and its tendency to fragment the social order into competing groups, had called into question the relevance of the old party structure, while the political elite's attempts at social engineering had provoked revolt. The unexpected weakening of the American economy also brought a new sense of limits and eased the return of conservative politics. But above all the post-war liberal consensus (and Democratic ascendancy) could not withstand the divisive issue of race and the souring impact of Vietnam.

In the past some measure of coherence had been preserved in national government because the party that held the presidency had usually also been in control of Congress, but by the time the 1960s were over American voters were no longer being so obliging. The turmoil of the decade undermined the partisanship that had preserved a measure of stability and also served to promote a popular distrust of politicians and of government. Political apathy and cynicism were part of the heritage of the Sixties, as many Americans became detached from the electoral process, although the experiences of the decade had also abetted the growth of a host of diverse interests operating outside the party framework. The zeitgeist of the 1960s had revealed a yearning for action, but this political activism also tended to provoke counter action, and stalemate was sometimes the result. Action meant confrontation, and disputes revolving around rights in a fragmented polity were not easily compromised.

PART 2

Politics at Home and Abroad

The actions taken by governments are crucial to an understanding of the 1960s. The ferment of the decade owed something to the liberal optimism radiating from Washington in its early years. The Democratic administrations of John Kennedy and Lyndon Johnson, in keeping with the temper of the times, believed that the powers of government could be used to promote the good society, and Richard Nixon too hoped to offer a sense of national direction from the White House. Political leaders were naturally receptive to those messages from the academic and research communities and journals of opinion to the effect that science and technology offered government new and powerful tools, that American resources were prodigious, and that the social sciences could supply detailed prescriptions for public policies. Many in government itched to exercise such beneficent power both at home and abroad, and in the public at large those with a similar understanding of the possibilities of government mobilised to bring pressure on Washington. Liberals helped to set the agenda for the 1960s but they were to find that they could not always control it.

Governmental actions, of course, are the outcome of complex processes, including jockeying between interests within an administration, the interplay between the different branches of government, and the impact of public opinion. Some public policies of the 1960s were to a significant degree the product of presidential initiatives or decisions, such as John Kennedy's commitment to the Peace Corps and to a moon shot and Lyndon Johnson's Great Society programmes. Crucial foreign policy decisions, especially over Vietnam, were also taken by the White House. It may be that other presidents would have taken the same decisions, for there was always a body of opinion in favour of each of them, but responsibility lay primarily with the particular incumbent of the Oval Office. As it happened, some of the most fateful decisions of the 1960s were taken by Lyndon Johnson. Other policies and decisions were largely reactive, as when a rattled Kennedy White House belatedly moved to accord civil rights a high priority. The actions of government were both shaped by and helped to shape the actions on the streets. Much of the radicalisation of political opinion on both right and left was the product of outrage with administration policies. Neither the racist populism of George Wallace nor the revolutionary course of the New Left can be understood without reference to actions taken in Washington.

Increasingly in this highly complex society Americans were coming to be ordered by national standards and regulations. Both the radicals and counter-cultural activists on the left and the old-fashioned conservatives on the right were dismayed by the remorseless advance of national bureaucracy, a process which did not stop with the election of the Nixon administration. Government programmes and Supreme Court decisions were tending to diminish the area of local autonomy, partly because the rights of American citizens did not always seem safe in the hands of racist officials in the South or of Mayor Daley's belligerent police in Chicago. But the regulatory impulse was a complicated one. It could move both liberals who wanted to curb the abuses of business and local officials and conservatives who wanted to contain federal expenditures, for it could be cheaper to address an issue by introducing new rules than by establishing a new programme. The liberalism of Kennedy and Johnson did not survive the decade, but there were to be some continuities into the kind of conservatism personified by Richard Nixon.

CHAPTER 3

The Politics of Hope:
From Kennedy to Johnson

In 1962 the historian Arthur Schlesinger, Jr. published a collection of essays entitled *The Politics of Hope*, in which he held out the prospect that the impulses of innovation in American life might burst forth and 'launch the United States into a new and more entertaining epoch'. Indeed, two years into the Sixties he believed that this renaissance was already happening, as illustrated by the young and energetic national leadership, the idealism of the Peace Corps, a new vigour in the arts, and even a healthy outbreak of satire. This was not to suggest that Americans were witnessing the dawning of a modern utopia, for the 'party of Hope' had 'no sense of messianic mission, ... no faith that fundamental problems have final solutions'. Rather, it was 'humane, skeptical, and pragmatic'; it held out the prospect of a better life for Americans, but not without struggle: 'Freedom is inseparable from struggle; it is a process, not a conclusion'. Other Americans in some measure shared these sentiments. In a survey taken in 1963 white and black Americans affirmed in general that they expected both their personal positions and the standing of the United States to improve over the next five years.

For Schlesinger the 'party of hope' was closely identified with the Kennedy administration. The values he was cherishing permeated the rhetoric of the New Frontier. Kennedy was not promising Americans a life of comfort. 'We will need in the sixties a President who is willing and able to summon his national constituency to its finest hour', he said in January 1960, '– to alert the people to our dangers and our opportunities – to demand of them the sacrifices that will be necessary.' This was his theme when he accepted the Democratic nomination. He invoked the struggle of the early pioneers to build a new world, arguing that the same spirit of self-sacrifice was needed to rise to the challenges of the new frontier: 'Beyond that frontier are uncharted areas of science and space, unsolved problems of peace and war, unconquered pockets of ignorance and prejudice, unanswered questions of poverty and surplus'. The times demanded 'innovation, imagination, decision', he said. 'I am asking each of you to be pioneers on that new frontier . . .' Courage, self-sacrifice, decisiveness – these were key words of the New Frontier. The new frontiersmen, to use Kennedy's phrase, would get the country 'moving again'. Progress might take time, Kennedy warned at his Inauguration: 'But let us begin'.

The Kennedy administration has sometimes been accused of raising expectations that could not be fulfilled, thus contributing to the embittered emergence of the New Left and black militancy. There is little doubt that the rhetoric of the New Frontier did lift hopes and inspire an idealism among many Americans that could not survive a brutal reality, but the Kennedy message was also that there were no easy solutions. Kennedy was throwing down a challenge, not promising utopia. It was his successor, Lyndon Johnson, who offered the most extravagant vision, confidently holding out the prospect of decisive victories over poverty and racism at home and communism abroad. But by the middle of the decade Johnson's optimism was straining credibility. Ghetto anger and the Vietnam quagmire were to prove fatal to the politics of hope.

What distinguished the Kennedy administration was not its commitment to reform but its commitment to action, or what Kennedy called 'vigor'. John Kennedy was no radical but he did believe that it was the duty of government to further the public good. What powerfully attracted many Americans to him was his identification with service rather than business; his very charm dispelled any notion that his interests were purely self-serving. Eisenhower's cabinet of 'nine businessmen and a plumber' and his rather conservative economic and social policies had conveyed the impression that domestically it was an administration's first duty to preserve an environment favourable to business and commerce. Kennedy's rhetoric, however, combined with his youth, suggested that there were other priorities. Many young people were moved by Kennedy's call, and saw in the New Frontier an opportunity to enlist in a cause of some worth. A significant number of these were to grow disenchanted in due course and enter the ranks of the New Left.

To deliver the stimulus that he believed the country needed, Kennedy was determined to gather round him 'the brightest and best people possible'. Those who joined the administration illustrated Kennedy's penchant for energy and a non-ideological commitment to public service. The average age of his cabinet (47) was ten years younger than that of Eisenhower, and into its most conspicuous positions were placed men of acknowledged competence. As Secretary of Defense there was Robert S. McNamara, the 'whiz kid' who had recently shot to the presidency of the Ford Motor Company and the reputed possessor of a formidable mind. Secretary of the Treasury was Douglas Dillon, like McNamara a Republican and one who had even served in the Eisenhower administration. But pragmatic and professional, Dillon would reassure the financial community as he worked to further Kennedy's expansionist policies. To the State Department went to Dean Rusk, a hardworking Georgian whose self-effacing demeanour suited a president who intended to be his own Secretary of State. As Attorney General the young president appointed his even younger brother Robert, who had master-minded his campaign and who would be his confidant in his official family. Liberal Democrats went to other cabinet posts. The emphasis on talent was reflected also in White House appointments. McGeorge Bundy, a near-legendary dean of Harvard, became Special Assistant for National Security Affairs. If Dillon's appointment had been designed to reassure Wall Street, a number of Keynesian economists were placed in other key economic positions, including economics professor Walter Heller as chair of the Council of Economic Advisers (CEA). When a somewhat awed Vice President Johnson relayed to his friend Sam Rayburn his impressions of the brilliance of the Kennedy men, Rayburn grumbled that 'they may be every bit as intelligent as you say, but I'd feel a whole lot better if just one of them had run for sheriff once'.

The press focus on the Kennedy White House, on 'Camelot', helped sustain the sense of excitement. The president's youth and energy, and his wife Jackie's beauty and interest in culture, served to attract talented men and women to Washington. Alfred Kazin commented of those around Kennedy that they gave 'the glow of those who have not merely conceived a great work but are in a position to finish it'. But the constraints on Kennedy were considerable – he had won election by a hairsbreadth and the conservative bloc in Congress was as powerful as ever – and his very pragmatism meant that the more fervent liberalism of some of his advisers held little appeal for him. Kennedy wanted action – but prudently. Not all his critics thought his activism wise. One joke in conservative circles before the end of Kennedy's administration was: 'Truman showed that anyone can be President, Ike that no one could be President, Kennedy that it can be dangerous to have a President'.

Action did not mean radicalism. The Kennedy men were impatient with what they saw as the torpidity of the Eisenhower presidency, but this did not mean that they favoured peace initiatives abroad or socialistic solutions at home. They were members of their generation, brought up on the Cold War, in which they wished to regain the initiative. This was to mean a build up of US armaments and greater involvement in the Third World (see Chapter 4). In economic policy, they looked to adopt the lessons of Keynes in managing the economy, and while this implied a more active role for government it did not imply disturbing the basic capitalist structure. In social policy they hoped to help the poor and distressed, although not in ways that might jeopardise either the nation's international stance or its economic growth.

Kennedy's disposition to combine prudence with action was illustrated in his economic policy. The shuffling of New Deal politics towards a commercial Keynesian position had begun in the Roosevelt and Truman administrations, as they came to deploy fiscal (tax and spend) methods of managing the economy in place of more regulatory techniques. It was the very failure of the Eisenhower administration to maximise the potential of the economy, with its dogged quest for balanced budgets, that exasperated many of the academic economists who offered their skills to Kennedy. But commercial Keynesianism was no radical creed. It did not look to a fundamental restructuring of the economy; it proposed no particular assault on the bastions of corporate power (though its practitioners were often wary of businessmen as self-serving and short-sighted); it had little enthusiasm for public ownership, and only a modest interest in public works or in measures to promote a redistribution of income. One way of stimulating the economy would be through tax cuts that put more money in the hands of consumers.

Even during a period of relative prosperity, it came to be argued, if there was slack in the economy it would be legitimate to run a government deficit in order to boost demand and thereby bring about stronger growth and full employment. This was the kind of argument used to justify the major tax cut that Kennedy proposed in 1963. There was no recession at the time, but the tax cut would enhance the purchasing power of consumers and spur greater economic activity. Faster growth in turn would lead to the increased government revenues needed to pay for activist domestic and foreign policies. Put another way, the theory was to invigorate the economy to the degree needed to support the enhanced government expenditure envisaged. If the economy overheated there would have to be moves to curb consumer demand in order to avert inflation, but Walter Heller and his colleagues hoped that by careful management they could keep both unemployment and inflation low.

Kennedy himself did not immediately embrace the new economics. His first tax changes involved depreciation allowances and investment tax credits, which may have been good for business but hardly appealed to his more liberal constituents. In June 1962 he used a public address at Yale to question the conventional wisdom about the need for balanced budgets and urged the priority of promoting economic growth. Finally, in January 1963 Kennedy submitted a budget incorporating tax cuts of $10.2 billion and called for tax reforms. In the event most of the reforms were removed by Congress, but it was the massive tax cut that the president most wanted, and by October 1963 the house of representatives had agreed to this.

In one sense the tax cut was conservative economics. The stimulus to the economy was not to be given by greater government spending but by leaving money in the hands of individuals and corporations, which suited the wealthy well enough. As one official later admitted, the cut 'didn't do a damn thing for poor people'. The action was to provide a precedent for future administrations, including the most conservative, and indeed budget deficits were to become the norm until the very end of the century. On the other hand, in 1963 Kennedy was flying in the face of fiscal orthodoxy, and the measure required vigorous drives to win over Congress, business, and public opinion. None of his predecessors had called for a large tax cut when the budget was already in deficit and the economy not in recession. After the measure passed in 1964 unemployment did drop and economic growth did speed up, much as predicted. But by the time the tax concessions took effect the economy was already gathering speed, so that the cut simply accelerated a boom rather than triggered it.

Through 'fine tuning' it was believed that economic growth could be secured without inflation, and among the techniques the administration used to contain the latter were wage and price guidelines. The 1950s had witnessed one of the great merger movements in American history, as smaller firms were taken over by larger ones. Business consolidation no longer worried liberals to the degree that it once had, but they were worried about price-fixing, particularly when a large corporation might act a price 'leader', setting a price for its products that other producers could follow. Kennedy's wage and price 'guideposts' illustrated his intent on more active economic management. The general message was that any wage and price increases should not exceed productivity gains. (One reason for the administration's concern over prices was the declining international competitiveness of the economy.) In practice, the guideposts meant that government officials would try to exhort union and corporation leaders into exercising restraint, or, as the phrase went, they would be 'jawboned' into compliance.

The test came in the crucial industry of steel. Kennedy asked the steel companies to absorb any wage increase, and the Secretary of Labor jawboned the union leaders into moderating their demands. In April 1962 US Steel signed a new contract with the union in which the wage increase was well within the guidepost. The administration was delighted, but four days later US Steel announced a price hike, and other steel companies followed suit. 'My father always told me that all businessmen were sons of bitches', Kennedy expostulated, in a line that reached the press (though he probably said 'steelmen'). The White House publicly went on the offensive, including a televised address by the president, and forced the steel companies to cancel their increase. Presidential prestige had been preserved, but this was the low point of the administration's relationship with business, which the White House was soon working hard to repair. Within a year the steel companies had quietly secured most of the price increases they wanted.

What Kennedy's economic policy did not do was provide much in the way of new domestic spending programmes. One early measure was a minimum wage bill, which, in raising the minimum wage and bringing many more workers within its aegis, was intended to help the low paid without direct costs to the Treasury. A bill did become law, although only after Congress had severely narrowed its scope. Kennedy was somewhat more successful with measures that constituted the origins of the War on Poverty. He had been distressed by what he had seen of poverty during his 1960 campaign, and the Area Redevelopment Act of 1961 provided for federal monies for regions of high unemployment. The Manpower Development and Training Act of 1962 was largely designed to ease people into jobs by providing them with training. Kennedy also persuaded Congress to increase funds to train social workers, and to extend federal welfare benefits to families with unemployed parents, although about half the states (which had to provide matching funds) declined to adopt the latter. Nonetheless, during the Kennedy administration and at the president's behest, Walter Heller's CEA had begun a study of the nature of poverty, something which (as distinct from unemployment) had not previously been seen as a federal responsibility.

Given Congress's long-standing resistance to liberal legislation, Kennedy's record on the domestic front was respectable enough, but it was disappointing in that he did not secure some of his most favoured measures. In 1961, for example, he failed to win congressional approval for two long-standing liberal proposals, providing for federal assistance for public (that is, state) schools and medical insurance for the elderly.

Kennedy was more successful with Congress in his expensive determination to put the United States ahead in the conquest of space. American prestige had suffered a major blow with the Soviet Sputnik of 1957, and Kennedy had slated the Eisenhower administration for allowing the United States to lag in the space race. A further humiliation had been suffered in April 1961 when Yuri Gagarin became the first man to orbit the earth. In May Kennedy told Congress that it was time for 'this nation to take a clearly leading role in space achievement, which in many ways may hold the key to our future on earth'. Whatever importance space exploration held for the future of humankind, it is doubtful whether the advancement of science would best be furthered by sending a man to the moon and back. But this is precisely what Kennedy asked for 'before the decade is out', although he was warned it would cost a massive $40 billion. 'We choose to go to the moon in this decade ... because that goal will serve to organize and measure the best of our energies and skills', he said in 1962, '... and "Because it is there".' Eisenhower had resisted the idea when it was put to him, and the Apollo programme became one of Kennedy's abiding legacies.

If Kennedy was eager to ask Congress for space appropriations, he was slower to ask it for civil rights legislation. A Massachusetts Democrat more attuned to labour than to race issues, Kennedy had never been a spokesman for civil rights, although he had signalled his sympathy for the cause in the 1960 campaign. For many northern politicians at this time civil rights was a matter for the South. They might sympathise with African Americans protesting against segregation, but they doubted the political wisdom of the federal authorities interfering in the domestic affairs of southern states. In any case, the Democratic party nationally depended on the votes of both northern blacks and southern whites and its leaders had no wish to offend either constituency.

The civil rights section of the Democratic platform in 1960 had emphasised executive action rather than legislation. It spoke of a new Attorney General 'vigorously' invoking the powers invested in him by existing law and of an administration committed to ending racial discrimination: 'Above all, it will require the strong, active, persuasive, and inventive leadership of the President of the United States'. Executive action, not new legislation, is what had been offered. The stress on executive action, of course, jibed with Kennedy's conception of an active presidency, as it contrasted with Eisenhower's reluctance to use such power. More to the point, Kennedy could not see how an ambitious civil rights bill could pass Congress. A mild bill had been passed in 1960, and its powers had yet to be fully explored. The conservative bloc in Congress was still capable of exercising its veto, and the election of 1960 had actually reduced Democratic majorities in both houses. Southern Democrats, for the most part committed to maintaining a segregated South, remained strongly entrenched in Congress, not least as chairs of major committees.

Kennedy saw little virtue in expending political capital in a probably fruitless confrontation with Congress over civil rights in 1961. But he did take executive action, more so than any previous president. Part of this was symbolic, such as increasing the number of African Americans in honour guards on ceremonial occasions. Some was more significant. Kennedy recruited more blacks to federal office than any of his predecessors. In his first two months he appointed Robert C. Weaver to head the Housing and Home Finance Agency, another forty African Americans to senior posts, and in September Thurgood Marshall, the leading lawyer of the National Association for the Advancement of Colored People, to the federal judiciary. The difficulty of securing civil rights legislation from Congress was illustrated when the Senate Judiciary Committee delayed Marshall's confirmation for a year. Kennedy also issued an executive order establishing the President's Committee on Equal Employment Opportunity, which prodded government departments and companies with federal contracts to give more jobs to blacks. More belated was Kennedy's executive order to end discrimination in federal housing facilities, which had been promised in the 1960 campaign but was delayed until after the mid-term elections of 1962. His attempts to work with the southern-dominated Senate Judiciary Committee also led to the appointment of a number of segregationists to federal judgeships in the South.

Enforcing existing civil rights legislation was the responsibility of the Justice Department, and it is one that Robert Kennedy took seriously. He had no wish for public confrontations with southern officials and worked hard behind the scenes to secure their compliance with the law, but his urgency in securing enforcement contrasted markedly with his predecessor. Where there was southern resistance, as in recognising black voting rights, Robert Kennedy regularly secured court orders. The Eisenhower Justice Department had initiated only six suits against the denial of voting rights to southern blacks; Robert Kennedy initiated fifty-seven. He also assisted in the establishment of the Voter Education Project in 1961, a co-operative enterprise by a number of groups to register southern blacks to vote. This endorsement of voter registration reflected a calculation to deflect civil rights activists from other forms of direct action, but undertaking this work in the Deep South was dangerous enough, and activists who were assaulted bitterly complained at the lack of federal protection. Kennedy was looking for a way of helping blacks without alienating the southern wing of the Democratic party, but these two goals were not easily compatible.

There were tensions between the Kennedy administration and the civil rights leadership, which had hoped for faster progress, but for the most part the principal civil rights groups felt that the administration was an ally, if a somewhat unreliable one, a novel situation in itself. The civil rights movement was growing in confidence (see Chapter 6). As it developed its techniques of non-violent direct action, often provoking a violent reaction from local segregationists, the Kennedy administration, with its claim to be the champion of freedom in the Cold War world, was obliged to respond. In May 1961 the Congress of Racial Equality (CORE), to the irritation of the administration, launched the Freedom Rides, when black and white students took bus rides into the South to challenge the continued segregation of bus stations. The buses were attacked by mobs in Alabama, the riders viciously beaten, and Robert Kennedy hurriedly despatched 400 (unarmed) federal marshals to protect them. CORE's use of direct action thus forced federal intervention, albeit of a restrained kind. The formal objective was won when the Attorney-General prevailed on the Interstate Commerce Commission to effect the integration of southern terminals, although he also urged a 'cooling-off' period on civil rights activists.

Another confrontation that the administration would have preferred to avoid was the 'Battle of Ole Miss' in 1962. Black air force veteran James Meredith was determined to study at the all-white University of Mississippi, and secured a court order requiring his admission. The Justice Department was responsible for enforcing the order, and again was obliged to intervene, directing a force of 500 marshals to protect Meredith. Marshals rather than troops were despatched in order to minimise the use of federal force, but the situation quickly deteriorated as white students and locals protested. A riot broke out in which two observers died, including a French newsman. The administration's attempt to 'manage' the crisis had proved inadequate, and the president was unhappily forced to deploy federal troops. 'Ole Miss' was thus forcibly integrated, and the affair did something to persuade the president of the need for federal power as well as negotiation in changing southern race relations. The reputation of the Kennedys in the Deep South sank to a new vituperative low, and was not helped in the following year when they faced down Governor George Wallace at the University of Alabama, where two black students were enrolled under federal protection though without violence. The administration could take some comfort from the thought that the issue at the University of Alabama had been peaceably resolved, although Wallace had garnered valuable publicity.

But crisis was brewing in Alabama. The civil rights movement itself was gaining momentum, probing for weak points in the edifice of segregation. In 1963 its pre-eminent leader, Martin Luther King Jr, determined to deploy his techniques of non-violent protest in Birmingham, Alabama. In a city whose police were controlled by the archsegregationist Bull Connor, the authorities lost patience with the demonstrators, particularly when King allowed black schoolchildren to join the protests, and resorted to the use of police dogs and high pressure fire hoses. Pictures of police dogs lunging at peaceful protestors flashed across television sets around the country. The atmosphere in Birmingham was further poisoned by the racist rhetoric of Alabama's governor, George Wallace. As racial violence flickered in the city in May 1963, the Kennedy administration redoubled its efforts, its negotiators trying to persuade local officials and businesses to desegregate.

By this date the White House had become persuaded of the need for a major initiative to regain its authority. It was finally being forced to choose between its African American and its southern white constituents. In February 1963 Kennedy had asked Congress for a moderate civil rights bill to strengthen black voting and educational rights, but the turmoil in Birmingham convinced him of the need for more far-reaching measures, particularly as hundreds of demonstrations erupted across the South, leading to thousands of arrests. How could federal authorities possibly protect all the demonstrators who were now taking to the streets? There was something close to panic in the administration as the country seemed to be spiralling out of control. In a televised speech on 11 June 1963 Kennedy said that federal legislation was needed 'if we are to move this problem from the streets to the courts'. It was a moral issue: 'We preach freedom around the world . . ., and we cherish our freedom here at home, but are we to say . . . that this is a land of the free except for the Negroes; that we have no second-class citizens except Negroes?' The administration submitted a sweeping civil rights bill to Congress and through the summer and autumn stretched every nerve to build support for it, winning the critical co-operation of congressional Republicans. The civil rights groups mobilised a mammoth March on Washington in August in support of the measure. President Kennedy cautiously declined to attend, but after the historic assembly had concluded peacefully he invited its organisers to the White House. John F. Kennedy had been primarily interested in foreign affairs when he was elected, but in the summer of 1963 it was the civil rights issue that was commanding his attention (partly because of what it might do to the international image of the United States). It was to remain for Lyndon Johnson to see the civil rights bill through Congress.

Kennedy's performance on civil rights did not enthral all blacks, but he could at least claim that he had provided leadership, that he had illustrated how some progress could be achieved through executive action, and that his administration had proposed the most far-reaching civil rights legislation since Reconstruction. By the summer of 1963 his understanding of the injustice suffered by African Americans had grown, and he was fighting to conduct the turbulent currents released by the issue along constructive channels. The authority of the presidency had been placed behind civil rights, and Kennedy used the various means at his disposal, including television, to mobilise public opinion for his policy. The White House also spent prodigious energy pleading and bargaining with the representatives of the white South, sometimes threatening legal action, as it also focused its powers of persuasion on southern business leaders (to have their businesses employ or serve blacks as well as to bring pressure to bear on city councils).

At times Kennedy was exasperated by the confrontational tactics of civil rights activists. For him politics was the art of the possible. Sometimes this meant concessions to southern white interests, and civil rights leaders were often offended by what they saw as half-hearted action by the White House. The CORE leader John Lewis described the civil rights bill as 'too little, too late'. Some African Americans became deeply embittered by the failure of the Kennedy administration to afford them the degree of protection and support they believed had been offered, engendering in them the distrust of liberal reform that was to become the premise of the Black Power movement. But most African Americans concluded that, whatever their failings, the Kennedys were more friends than foes of the civil rights cause and there is little doubt that had John Kennedy lived to contest the 1964 election he would have won the overwhelming support of black voters. He would also have run badly in the white South. In February 1963 Kennedy's approval rating in the South had been 70 per cent; by the end of June, after King's Birmingham campaign and the president's public commitment to a strong civil rights bill, it had plunged to 33 per cent.

John Kennedy's assassination in November 1963 shocked peoples everywhere. The hope that this young and charismatic leader had personified, both for his country and for the wider world, was momentarily shaken. But shocking as it was, the murder interrupted rather than arrested the cause of liberal reform. The new president, Lyndon Johnson, pressed Kennedy's appointees to remain at their posts and he committed himself to delivering the promises of the slain leader.

In some respects the new president contrasted sharply with his predecessor. A massive Texan, he was earthy, overbearing and desperately insecure, insisting that he wanted aides around him who would 'kiss my ass on a summer's day and say it smelled like roses'. Yet the contrast with Kennedy was mainly in personality. Like Kennedy, Johnson could be classified as a liberal Democrat. Like Kennedy, he saw the presidency as an office in which leadership could and should be asserted, and he too believed in action. He shared the 'can do' mentality of the Kennedy men, and if anything was more convinced than they that every problem had its solution. He also shared the Cold War assumptions of Kennedy and of their generation of political leaders.

But Johnson also brought to the presidency certain attributes of his own. He had spent twenty-three years in Congress, consummating his remarkable career there as majority leader in the senate. As much the most powerful figure on Capitol Hill, Johnson at times could almost be seen as prime minister to Dwight Eisenhower's ailing constitutional monarch, although their party differences limited their co-operation. Johnson the wheeler-dealer knew the corridors of congressional power intimately. The vice presidency allowed only limited scope for his ambitions, but Kennedy's death precipitated into the presidency a man of extraordinary energy. His commitment to reform was also stronger than Kennedy's, for Johnson had been a keen supporter of Franklin Roosevelt's New Deal, and if he saw himself as the legatee of the Kennedy programme, he also saw himself as the heir of Roosevelt. 'He was like a daddy to me', said Johnson of Franklin D. Roosevelt. But he craved an even better reform record than his hero.

While Johnson's crudeness and southern roots made him a suspect figure to some liberals, others recognised that he could powerfully strengthen the reform cause. The elemental force of his personality, his legendary understanding of Congress, his ambition for accomplishments, and his own empathy for the underdog augured well for 'the party of hope'. In his first speech to Congress, a few days after the assassination, Johnson evoked memories of Kennedy's Inaugural: 'Today, in this moment of new resolve, I would say to all my fellow Americans, *let us continue*'.

The two most important pieces of unfinished legislative business left over from the Kennedy administration were the tax cut and the civil rights bill. Johnson early made clear his commitment to these measures. To secure the unorthodox tax cut Johnson effected a slight bow towards conservative apprehensions by making a modest budget reduction, and he was able to sign the bill into law in February 1964. He was even more determined to see the civil rights bill through Congress without weakening amendments, and after the longest filibuster in Senate history it became law in the summer of 1964. (See Chapter 6 for its impact.) Johnson, of course, was aided by the way in which public opinion rallied behind Kennedy's programme in the aftermath of his murder, but the president's consummate legislative skills also ensured that these measures were not fatally compromised in Congress.

Kennedy's aides had also been talking about measures to attack poverty, although at the time of Kennedy's death no clear proposal had been formulated. Told by Walter Heller of these discussions, Johnson responded: 'That's my kind of programme. We should push ahead full-tilt on this project.' An anti-poverty crusade jibed with Johnson's New Deal values, and offered him an opportunity to put his own imprint on the presidency. 'This administration today, here and now, declares unconditional war on poverty in America,' he said in his State of the Union Address in January 1964, just two months into his presidency. The War on Poverty, explained *Nation* magazine, originated in 'an almost mystical belief in the infinite potentials of American society'. Johnson named the energetic Peace Corps Director Sargent Shriver to head the offensive and by March Shriver had a prepared a bill. The Economic Opportunity Act duly became law in August, a hastily-contrived package authorising a range of projects. It created an Office of Economic Opportunity (OEO) to oversee the diverse measures. The programme was grounded largely on the assumption that education was the escalator to lift people out of poverty – the poor needed 'a hand up, not a hand out'. Head Start was to offer nursery education for deprived children and Upward Bound sought to make it possible for them to reach higher education; the Job Corps provided job training for ghetto youngsters; a domestic equivalent of the Peace Corps was established in the form of the Volunteers in Service to America (VISTA). The most controversial part of the package was the Community Action Program (CAP), which reflected the belief that the poor themselves should have some say in their own salvation and which was designed to encourage local communities to undertake their own programmes.

Johnson had promised that the War on Poverty would be 'unconditional' and he apparently believed that with the right measures poverty could be eradicated. But while the programme might ameliorate poverty, its design was flawed if the aim was to abolish it. Too little money was spent. The OEO's initial budget of $960 million might be compared to the $4.5 billion allocated to Franklin Roosevelt's Works Progress Administration in 1935, or to the $50 billion of military spending in 1965. While the OEO's yearly appropriation crept up to an average of about $1.7 billion, that was only about 1.5 per cent of the federal budget. The strategy for fighting poverty was also poorly planned. The emphasis on education (rather than jobs or cash payments) made political sense, since the programme could be justified in terms of fulfilling the American ideal of equality of opportunity, and Congress is unlikely to have approved anything more ambitious, but it largely ignored the economic basis of poverty. In any case, equipping people for the urban job market was of limited use to the underpaid, single mothers and the elderly. Many of the projects were not thought through, partly because Johnson was anxious to speed his measures through Congress while it was still amenable to reform. Unsurprisingly, the War on Poverty met with mixed results. Parts of it, such as Head Start and Upward Bound, seemed reasonably successful; other programmes, such as the Job Corps, proved disappointing. Many of the CAPs functioned well, improving social services in local communities, but the requirement that the poor participate in their management precipitated howls of protest from established city officials. In some places the struggle for the control of the CAPs set white politicians against black radicals and exacerbated racial tensions.

But Johnson's ambition was almost limitless. By May 1964 the War on Poverty had expanded into something even bolder, when in a speech at the University of Michigan Johnson spoke of the Great Society, which 'demands an end to poverty and racial injustice. ... But that is just the beginning'. It was also a society where 'every child can find knowledge to enrich his mind', where 'the city of man serves not only the needs of his body and the demands of commerce but the desire for beauty and the hunger for community'. But 'most of all' the Great Society was 'a challenge constantly renewed, beckoning us toward a destiny where the meaning of our lives matches the marvelous products of our labor'. Johnson seemed to be promising reform without end, and certainly a mighty monument by which his administration would be remembered. Where Kennedy had promised action, Johnson promised massive social reform.

For a couple of years Johnson's bills tumbled through Congress, facilitated by the Democratic sweep in the 1964 elections. Not only was Johnson unequivocally elected president in his own right, but large Democratic majorities were secured in both houses of Congress, overwhelming the conservative bloc that had obstructed reform legislation for decades. Between 1965 and 1968 some 500 social programmes were launched, the most important measures coming in 1965. Johnson would claim that, despite the flaws that were revealed, his various Great

Society measures together had considerable impact. The number of Americans below the poverty line fell from 33 to 25 million between 1965 and 1970 (or from 17 to 13 per cent), although a significant and unknown part of this improvement must have been a product of the expanding economy. Other than in World War Two, poverty had never diminished so fast.

In 1965 Medicare provided health insurance for the elderly, and Medicaid offered health services to those on welfare. The existing major federal welfare programme, Aid for Families with Dependent Children (AFDC) was enhanced, and food stamp and school lunch programmes were greatly expanded. A major innovation was achieved with the Elementary and Secondary Schools Act, designed to channel federal money into schools in poor neighbourhoods, because the school systems had previously been the preserve of the states. 'He was a nut on education', recalled Hubert Humphrey of Lyndon Johnson. 'He felt that education was the greatest thing he could give to the people; he just believed in it, just like some people believe in miracle cures.' The Higher Education Act followed in the same year, providing funds for certain programmes and especially for scholarships and loans for students. In September Johnson also secured congressional approval for the establishment of a new cabinet department, the Department of Housing and Urban Development, and a few months later appointed the first black cabinet member, Robert Weaver, to head it. Environmental reform too resurfaced as a liberal cause, which the president furthered by securing a Highway Beautification Act and also a pair of water quality and clean air acts. Some of these measures, like Medicare, were of more service to the middle class than to the poor.

Civil rights was still on the agenda, commanding national attention by Martin Luther King's campaign in Selma, Alabama, to force the local authorities to register black residents. King's design was also to bring pressure to bear on the White House and Congress for a voting rights bill. The civil rights act of 1964 had been focused on desegregation, but in many southern states blacks were still largely excluded from the voting registers. King's confrontational strategy in Selma worked, the violent behaviour of local white officials prompting repudiation from Washington. A determined Lyndon Johnson dramatically addressed a joint session of Congress in a televised speech. 'Their cause must be our cause too . . .', he declared in an impassioned plea for the bill, punctuating his speech by raising his arms and proclaiming the rallying cry of the civil rights movement: 'We shall overcome'. Watching on television, Martin Luther King was moved to tears. In August 1965 Johnson symbolically signed the bill into law in the same room in which Abraham Lincoln had signed the Emancipation Proclamation.

Johnson's legislative accomplishments were awesome. 'Johnson has outstripped Roosevelt, no doubt about that', observed Senate Majority Leader Mike Mansfield. 'He has done more than FDR ever did or ever thought of doing'. Like Roosevelt's innovations, Johnson expected his programmes to grow over time. 'I figured when my legislative program passed the Congress that the Great Society had a real chance to grow into a beautiful woman', he recalled to Doris Kearns in 1971. 'And I figured her growth and development would be as natural and inevitable as any small child's:'

> In the first year, as we got the laws on the books, she'd begin to crawl. Then in the second year, as we got more laws on the books, she'd begin to walk, and the year after that, she'd be off and running, all the time growing bigger and fatter and healthier. And when she grew up, I figured she'd be so big and beautiful that the American people couldn't help but fall in love with her, and once they did, they'd want to keep her around forever, making her a permanent part of American life, more permanent even than the New Deal.

Johnson would have liked to concentrate his energies on his 'beautiful woman', but Vietnam was increasingly commanding his attention. Not only was the war guzzling resources, but its escalation during 1965 strained Johnson's relationships with many reform allies. By this time several Kennedy men had left the administration. The most symbolic breach was with Robert Kennedy, who quit the cabinet in August 1964 and who was soon elected to represent New York in the senate. The optimism that many liberals had felt in the early 1960s was beginning to evaporate.

But Lyndon Johnson was facing criticism on the right as well as on the left. Already there was the beginning of a backlash against civil rights and Great Society policies. Johnson had won a landslide victory in 1964, but there had been some defections among normally Democratic voters, and at the end of that year, when asked their attitude towards welfare programmes, some 45 per cent of those polled reported 'mixed feelings' as against 43 per cent who were 'favorable'. The summer race riots of 1964 and 1965, particularly the Watts riot of

August 1965, suggested that that the liberal dream of integration was an illusion. They fostered the impression that black militants were bent on bringing race war into the northern cities. In March a Gallup Poll had asked respondents whether the administration was pushing integration too fast, but 38 per cent thought the pace 'about right' against 34 per cent who thought it 'too fast'; during the summer the 'too fast' figure overtook the 'about right' figure.

Johnson's foreign policy was also coming under attack. At the same time as he going to war for his Great Society Johnson was going to war in Asia, and anti-war sentiment was mounting. It was in February 1965 that Johnson initiated the bombing of North Vietnam and by July he was embarking on the massive escalation of troops in Vietnam. It was foreign policy in particular that generated talk of a 'credibility gap' in 1965, as Johnson's exaggerated rhetoric and attempt to control the flow of news raised doubts as to how far he was telling the truth. Some of Johnson's aides began to fear for his mental stability, as in private he on occasion represented himself as a victim of a massive communist conspiracy. By November 1965 the Council of Economic Advisors was becoming worried about the economic impact of the accelerating defence expenditures.

'I knew from the start', Johnson told biographer Doris Kearns in 1970, 'that I was bound to be crucified either way I moved:'

> If I left the woman I really loved – the Great Society – in order to get involved with that bitch of a war on the other side of the world, then I would lose everything at home. All my programs. All my hopes to feed the hungry and shelter the homeless. . . . But if I left that war and let the Communists take over South Vietnam, then I would be seen as a coward and my nation would be seen as an appeaser and we would both find it impossible to accomplish anything for anybody anywhere in the entire globe.

Broadly public opinion still backed Johnson over Vietnam, but there were doubts about its solidity. One official reported in December: 'The polls give the President high marks on Vietnam – but I have a vague feeling that this support may be more superficial than it is deep and committed (many people do not even understand what it is they are supporting)'. By the end of the year opinion polls showed that 'Vietnam' had displaced 'civil rights' as the 'most important problem' in the public mind. And Johnson's own standing was beginning to erode. At the beginning of 1965 Johnson's approval rating in the polls had been 71 per cent; by the end of the year it had slipped to 62 per cent. This was still a respectable figure, much the same as John Kennedy's in the last months of his life, but the honeymoon was over.

The honeymoon with reform was largely over too. The Kennedy and Johnson administrations had offered Americans presidential leadership. Liberal and for the most part pragmatic, these were presidents who believed that the government could deliver, that it possessed the expertise and resources to secure its main objectives. They were to prove a point when they catapulted the United States to the fore in the space race. Their hands forced by the civil rights movement, their administrations delivered mortal blows to the segregationist South, as their measures also improved the lot of millions of the urban poor. But these achievements were secured at a cost, and by 1965 liberal activism seemed to be reaching its limits.

The attempt of the Kennedy administration to revitalise the American sense of mission now seemed to have been tempting fate. The New Frontier had been a call to a new generation to enlist in the service of their country and of humankind. John Kennedy had asked for self-sacrifice and had promised executive action and a cool head. True to his pledge, Kennedy had pursued an assertive foreign policy, as the next chapter will detail, but its results had been ambiguous and it had increased American commitments abroad. A rueful Arthur Schlesinger was to observe in the 1980s that the 'besetting sin of the New Frontier ... was the addiction of activism'. Kennedy's 'new' economic policy could claim some success, but the prospect of liberalised policies with respect to welfare and especially civil rights had served to raise expectations that could not easily be fulfilled, while the administration's caution on domestic issues could seem to activists to be a betrayal of the reform cause. Lyndon Johnson embraced reform with greater enthusiasm, but his extraordinary Great Society measures, coming as they did at a time of urban turmoil, encountered an emerging resistance among the white middle and even lower classes. Further, the escalating war in Vietnam threatened both the completion of Johnson's reform agenda and the bases of his political support. The summer of ghetto unrest of 1965 underlined the intractability of such issues as race and poverty, and for some liberals the 'politics of hope' were being replaced by something akin to despair.

CHAPTER 4

The United States in the World: From Hubris to Humiliation

At the outset of the 1960s much of the western world saw the international role of the United States as constructive and mostly benign. The United States, after all, had recently helped to save Europe from Nazi domination, and was again standing tall as a sentinel, guaranteeing 'western civilisation' against another totalitarian threat. In the post-war years, many European intellectuals and commentators who had previously scorned the pretensions of American culture had come to accept, in the words of Winston Churchill, that 'our future depends on our being mixed-up together with the Americans'. In Italy one group of scholars turned to the study of the United States for clues on how to develop pluralistic and democratic institutions. French sociologists, engineers, and journalists were intrigued by the highly visible 'modernity' of the United States. For some Europeans, particularly British commentators, the very fate of civilization seemed to rest with the American giant. In the immediate post-war years the fear was not so much that the United States might misuse its power; the fear was that it might not use it at all. In 1960 the British historian W. R. Brock wrote that in the twentieth century 'America is no longer required to reject Europe but to save it'. The affairs of the American people, he noted, had become intertwined with those of peoples everywhere; and it remained to be seen 'whether the intellectual and emotional resources of American civilization are sufficient to the times'. These cordial attitudes were not so widely found in Africa and Asia, and by the end of the 1960s many Europeans had abandoned them too. But early in the decade it was possible to see American power as a progressive force.

Many Americans too believed that the United States now possessed the opportunity, indeed the obligation, to play a constructive and

70

benign role in the world. John Kennedy was one of them. 'Let every nation know ... that we shall pay any price, bear any burden ... to assure the survival and the success of liberty', he said in his Inaugural Address: 'Now the trumpet summons us again ... to bear the burden of a long twilight struggle ... against the common enemies of man: tyranny, poverty, disease and war itself.' In his first State of the Union Message he added: 'The hopes of mankind rest upon us'. It was in foreign policy that the activist zeal animating the Kennedy men was most apparent. They believed that the Eisenhower regime had been too passive in its conduct of the Cold War, particularly in the arena that was assuming greater importance in that ideological conflict, the Third World. 'Euphoria reigned'; recalled Arthur Schlesinger as the Kennedy administration took office: 'we thought for a moment that the world was plastic and the future unlimited'.

The Kennedy and Johnson administrations were to find that the world was far from malleable. Before his early death a sobered Kennedy had begun to speak of making the world safe for 'diversity' rather than for democracy or freedom, and an inability to impose the American will in Southeast Asia was to drive President Johnson from the White House. By that date the intractable American involvement in Vietnam seemed to be both imperialist and racist to a growing number of Americans, as well as to many people around the world. The costly humiliation in a distant jungle did not cause the United States to revert to isolationism, as some thought it might, but it did precipitate an unhappy debate over her proper international role.

John Kennedy's Inaugural Address was almost entirely devoted to foreign affairs, reflecting both his personal interest and his vision of the United States as a beacon for humankind. 'My fellow citizens of the world:' he said, 'ask not what America will do for you, but what together we can do for the freedom of man'. Kennedy's itch for action meant that his presidency would not neglect its global responsibilities. One White House security aide, Walt Rostow, claimed that the move from Eisenhower to the Kennedy represented 'a shift from defensive reaction to initiative'.

During the 1960 campaign the Democrats had made much of the 'missile gap', yet another illustration of the Eisenhower administration's sluggishness, but on coming into office they discovered that the 'gap' was in favour of the United States. Still, Kennedy was uneasy about the degree to which the Eisenhower strategy had depended on the deterrence of nuclear weapons, and local tensions around the globe suggested that what was needed was a more 'flexible response'. Kennedy promptly launched a dramatic arms build-up, in March 1961 asking Congress to increase the defence budget, and in May, in the same message calling for the moon programme, he requested even greater monies for the armed forces, vulnerable regimes abroad, and civil defence. Funding these huge costs was one reason why faster economic growth was needed. On defence issues Congress was willing enough to align itself with the patriotic side, and defence expenditures increased by 13 per cent during the Kennedy administration. Flexible response meant that the United States was less dependent on threatening the use of nuclear weapons, although the implication was that military intervention abroad would increase, as indeed happened. According to one study, Kennedy deployed the armed forces more frequently than any other president in the thirty years after the Second World War, if not as heavily as some.

Kennedy wanted nuclear superiority too. As well as an enhanced conventional capability, the number of Intercontinental Ballistic Missiles (Minutemen) was doubled and Polaris submarines increased by 50 per cent. But what had been started could not easily be stopped. The Soviet Union could not allow the United States to gain an overwhelming superiority and threw itself desperately into producing more missiles of its own, obliging the United States in turn to increase its commitment. The Democratic criticism of Eisenhower for tolerating a missile gap had helped to precipitate an unnerving arms race.

The president's 'can do' philosophy was combined with a conviction that toughness was essential. In contemplating a meeting with the Soviet premier, Nikita Khrushchev, Kennedy insisted that 'I have to show him that we can be as tough as he is'. The two met in June 1961 in Vienna, where Khrushchev's belligerence shook the young president. The Soviet premier contemptuously spurned Kennedy's proposals that the existing balance of power (which greatly favoured the United States) should be preserved, and spoke of his support for 'wars of national liberation' in Third World countries subject to western control. Khrushchev reiterated the Soviet demand that the western powers quit West Berlin (through which refugees from the Communist East were streaming), which would become part of East Germany. Kennedy returned home determined to stand firm, but through the summer Khrushchev kept up the pressure for a Berlin settlement. 'All Europe is at stake in West Berlin', was Kennedy's view and he refused to yield, dramatically going on television to call for increased spending on civil defence because of the possibility of nuclear war and asking Congress to increase the military budget immediately by \$3.2 billion. Yet he also seemed to be implying that the West had no vital stake in East Berlin, and this gave the Soviet Union a way out of the impasse – in August the Berlin Wall was built to shut the East off from the West, thus stopping the embarrassing flow of refugees. The United States tacitly accepted this solution, thus also tacitly accepting the continued division of Germany.

Khrushchev may have spoken of 'wars of national liberation' at Vienna, but Kennedy himself was not insensitive to Third World problems. One of his criticisms of the Eisenhower administration was that it had been overly wedded to a bipolar view of the world, paying too little heed to the way in which European decolonisation and economic development in the Third World were changing global configurations of power. Of course, Kennedy was himself very much a disciple of the Cold War, and a significant part of his interest in the Third World was related to his desire not to see it succumb to Soviet influence. But he also recognised that nationalism was a powerful modern phenomenon, and he sought to align the United States with it. One illustration of this was his sustained support for the United Nations in the Congo, in an attempt to prevent that country's dismemberment. Often enough, however, Kennedy's interest in protecting Third World nationalism was compromised by Cold War considerations.

In Latin America, a White House aide advised Kennedy, 'the atmosphere is set for miracles'. In his Inaugural Address Kennedy had offered a 'special pledge' to the Latin American nations 'in a new alliance for progress – to assist free men and free governments in casting off the chains of poverty'. At the same time he warned off 'every other power' from interfering in 'this hemisphere'. In 1959 the pro-American regime in Cuba, which had long been a virtual dependency of the United States, was overthrown by Fidel Castro, who responded to US hostility by seizing American property in Cuba and establishing friendly relations with the Soviet Union. The sudden perception of the Cuban Revolution as a Communist one, and Castro's own boasts about his capacity to export revolution, raised the spectre of other impoverished Latin American countries following the Cuban example.

One possible response was for the United States to extend economic aid to Latin American nations and to encourage their regimes to develop in directions compatible with American economic and political philosophy. In August 1961 the Alliance for Progress was established to promote the economic development of Latin America, with the United States promising vastly increased financial aid, in return for internal reforms liberalising tax systems and land distribution. To Kennedy, as he privately explained it, this was a programme 'which I believe can successfully counter the Communist onslaught in this hemisphere'. The Alliance was to prove a disappointing experiment, at least in the promotion of social reform, but it was a sign of the administration's determination to gain the initiative in foreign affairs.

The Castro regime also provoked a more direct response. President Eisenhower had authorised the Central Intelligence Agency (CIA) to prepare a force of Cuban exiles to invade the island, in the hope of triggering a popular uprising against Castro. Kennedy permitted the invasion to go ahead in April 1961, though – deciding that US forces should not be directly involved – withheld air cover. The Bay of Pigs operation was a disaster, as the invaders were quickly defeated. 'Nobody in the White House wanted to be soft ...', said an aide. 'Everybody wanted to show they were just as daring and bold as everybody else'. The humiliation over the Bay of Pigs served to make the Kennedys even more determined to destroy Castro. Latin American governments were encouraged to break off diplomatic relations with Cuba, and Operation Mongoose was secretly launched, involving sabotage attempts on Cuban property. The CIA concluded it had licence to plot the assassination of Castro.

The harassment of Castro could only serve to push Cuba closer to the Soviet Union, which in 1962 tried to turn the situation to its own advantage by provocatively installing medium-range missiles on the island. That there was some kind of Soviet activity in Cuba was clear enough, and Republicans began to attack the administration for allowing the island to become a Soviet base. Then in October US reconnaissance planes photographed a missile launch pad under construction. The presence of Soviet missiles in Cuba would not have much altered the balance of power, but Kennedy would have great difficulty in persuading the American public of this, and in any case considered it dangerous to display weakness to the Soviet Union. 'This is reprise on the Bay of Pigs business and this time there will be no charges that somebody weakened at the crucial moment', one government official noted in his diary. The momentous confrontation took place. Kennedy took to television and starkly warned the Soviet Union that any nuclear missile launched from Cuba would provoke a full response by the United States directly on the Soviet Union. Kennedy's military advisers favoured an air strike on the missile bases, but he decided on a naval blockade of the island, to prevent Soviet ships from getting through. At the critical point the Soviet vessels turned back. Kennedy further publicly demanded that the Soviets dismantle the missiles, while Khrushchev was also given privately to understand that US missiles in Turkey would be removed. The Soviet premier bowed to Kennedy's public demand, and the threat of nuclear war was averted.

Kennedy emerged from the Cuban missile crisis with a considerably enhanced stature, at least in the United States. While there were critics of his actions, he generally was credited with responding to the crisis in a cool, rational and imaginative way. Further, he had faced the Soviet Union down, secured the initiative in the Cold War, and had shown the world that the United States would not be humiliated. But his need to demonstrate his toughness both to the American public and to Khrushchev had taken the world to the brink of nuclear war. Further, the crisis weakened the western alliance, for it suggested to European leaders that the United States would pay them minimal attention when it had its own reasons for acting. The French president, General de Gaulle, announced his intention of having France quit the North Atlantic Treaty Organisation.

Having looked over the brink, John Kennedy turned to ways of easing US-Soviet tensions. Both the Soviet premier and the American president began to show greater interest in a ban on nuclear testing, and in a speech at American University in June 1963 Kennedy stressed that the United States did not want 'a Pax Americana enforced on the world by American weapons of war'. He pointed out that there were alternatives to stockpiling weapons to keep the peace, suggested that conflict with the Soviets was not necessarily inevitable, and looked to an ending of the arms race. He also took the occasion to announce the establishment of a 'hot line' between Washington and Moscow to avoid dangerous misunderstandings. Kennedy suspended US atmospheric nuclear tests, and in August the two powers signed the nuclear test ban pact, renouncing testing above ground level.

If Kennedy was looking for a way of promoting peaceful co-existence, by 1963 he had come to appreciate the limits of American power. In disavowing a Pax Americana he was also acknowledging that the United States could not impose its values on other peoples. By this time the goal was the less imperialistic one of making 'the world safe for diversity'. Kennedy's mood in his final press conference struck a contrast with that of his Inauguration: 'I think it is a very dangerous, untidy world. I think we will have to live with it'. Perhaps decisive action was becoming less appealing to him. The world, particularly the Third World, was proving an intractable place.

The competition for the allegiance of the Third World precluded any real chance of accord. Since the Second World War European imperialism had been in retreat before the nationalist movements of Asia and Africa, but Big Power policy-makers too readily assumed that Third World aspirations should be seen in a Cold War perspective. 'The great battleground for the defense and expansion of freedom today is the whole southern half of the globe', Kennedy had said, '. . . the lands of the rising people'. In his Inaugural Address he had referred to 'those peoples in the huts and villages of half the globe struggling to break the bonds of mass misery', pledging them US assistance 'to help themselves', not 'because the Communists may be doing it . . . but because it is right'. But communist activity (or what could be mistaken for it) in the Third World undoubtedly disturbed Kennedy, particularly in Southeast Asia. The Truman administration had been seriously damaged by the 'loss' of China to the communists, and ever since the United States had been anxious to contain further communist advances in the region. The former French Indochina in particular seemed subject to communist subversion, despite the financial aid that the United States had been sending. It had also become an axiom among American policy-makers that the 'fall' of Indochina would lead to the communist control of the whole of Southeast Asia, and in due course of India and even Japan too. The 'domino theory' required the protection of the most exposed domino.

At the time of Kennedy's accession, there were 685 US military advisors in South Vietnam. The country was ruled by Ngo Dinh Diem, who had been facing a rebellion from the so-called Viet Cong (though many of these rebels were not communists). The rebels formed the National Liberation Front (NLF) to serve as their political arm, assisted by the leader of North Vietnam, Ho Chi Minh. To Secretary of State

Dean Rusk, the Diem regime in the South was the victim of aggression instigated by communist North Vietnam, which in turn was relying on China. Vietnam, he warned, must not become another Munich.

There was little likelihood of the Kennedy administration abandoning Vietnam. For one thing, Kennedy thought that he had the means of turning around the situation. He believed that Eisenhower had been unable to respond adequately to Soviet moves because the United States had become too dependent on the nuclear deterrent. What was needed was the capacity for a 'flexible response', which implied supplementing nuclear weapons with a substantial range of conventional weapons, and not least a capacity to wage guerrilla warfare. The insurgency that the Soviet Union seemed to be encouraging in the Third World could be seen off by counter-insurgency.

Kennedy's interest in counter-insurgency was illustrated by the attention he paid to the American Special Forces units, or Green Berets, which he expanded fivefold. This was an elite corps, specially trained and equipped with the latest technology. With such American expertise, local forces would be trained and assisted, and, together with political and social reforms, the threat of communist rebellion would be contained. Counter-insurgency would have the further advantage of avoiding a direct confrontation with the Soviet Union. Vice president Johnson was despatched to Vietnam to assess the situation. 'The basic decision in Southeast Asia is here', he reported back. 'We must decide whether to help these countries to the best of our ability or throw in the towel in the area and pull back our defenses to San Francisco and a "Fortress America" concept.' Encouraged by his advisors, Kennedy increased financial and military aid to the Diem regime, despite the latter's resistance to economic and political reform. By November 1963 there were 16,700 US military personnel in Vietnam, almost a 25-fold increase during the Kennedy presidency, though the president resisted military requests for combat troops.

In that month Diem was the victim of a military coup, one acquiesced in by the United States, which had become impatient with the ineffectiveness of the South Vietnam government. The Americans were doing more than advising that government; they were now involved in making it. A few weeks later Kennedy himself was assassinated. It is possible, as some of his advisors later claimed, that had he lived Kennedy might have found a way of disengaging from Vietnam before the US commitment became massive. But whatever he might have done, his successor by temperament was unlikely to lead a voluntary retreat. 'I am not going to lose Vietnam,' said Lyndon Johnson. 'I am not going to be the President who saw Southeast Asia go the way China went.'

During Johnson's first several months in office the war dragged on frustratingly, with the unstable South Vietnam regimes unable to strike effectively at the Viet Cong, and with Johnson both unwilling to withdraw and unwilling to commit US combat forces. In early August, however, North Vietnamese torpedo boats opened fire on US destroyers in the Gulf of Tonkin (or so the rather murky evidence suggested). Characterising the incident as open and deliberate aggression against the United States, while omitting to mention the assistance the destroyers were giving to South Vietnamese raids on the North Vietnam coast, Johnson asked Congress for a resolution giving him authority to take 'all necessary steps' to protect any nation protected by the South East Asia Treaty Organisation. Johnson wanted congressional endorsement for any escalation of the war. The vital resolution was passed unanimously by the house and with only two dissenting votes by the senate. Johnson also ordered an air strike against North Vietnamese torpedo boat bases.

This response helped Johnson ward off Republican charges of weakness over Vietnam during the presidential campaign of 1964, but he continued to resist a 'wider war'. He told his fellow Americans in the autumn that he was not 'ready for American boys to do the fighting for Asian boys'. His Republican opponent, Barry Goldwater, for his part castigated Johnson for 'a policy of weakness, a policy of indecision, a policy of indirection'.

In the early months of 1965 Johnson finally lost patience with the apparently endless policy of propping up ineffective governments in Vietnam. He had hitherto resisted advice to strike at the North while there was an unstable regime in the South, but he now began to calculate that increased pressure on Hanoi might serve to stiffen South Vietnamese resolve. When eight US advisors were killed in a Viet Cong attack on an American base, Johnson responded with an air attack on a North Vietnam army base. In mid-February 'Rolling Thunder' was launched without announcement, a bombing campaign that in the event lasted three years. As columnist James Reston put it, the United States had embarked on 'an undeclared and unexplained war in Vietnam'. Johnson doubted whether the bombing would do much to deter Hanoi, but he hoped that at least it would help to avert a collapse of the South Vietnam government. 'Light at the end of the tunnel,' he muttered to an aide. 'Hell, we don't even have a tunnel; we don't even know where the tunnel is.'

There were still only 23,000 military advisers in Vietnam, an increase on what Johnson had inherited from Kennedy but hardly an overwhelming number. In February, however, Johnson agreed to send US Marines to guard the American air base at Denang although not to send them into combat. But American commitment was almost imperceptibly growing. Johnson soon expanded the bombing, increased the number of military advisers, sent another couple of marine divisions, and, more significantly, by early April allowed the marines to shift to offensive operations. And with the bombing emerged increasing liberal criticism, to the surprise of the White House, which had previously been more subject to criticism from the right.

In a speech at Johns Hopkins University in March Johnson defended his Vietnam policy, insisting that the American presence was vital to containing communism in Asia. Hanging over the conflict, insisted Johnson, was 'the deepening shadow of Communist China'. But he also called on the North Vietnamese to enter peace talks, promising that if Hanoi guaranteed the independence of South Vietnam, the United States would pour a billion dollars into the area: 'The vast Mekong River can provide food and water and power on a scale to dwarf even our own TVA'. Hanoi was not interested and Johnson's critics were hardly reassured, but the broadly favourable public response to the speech helped to steel him to further action.

Reports from Vietnam indicated that the US Marines were inflicting far greater damage on the Viet Cong than the Vietnamese forces had ever achieved, evidence that suggested that only the deployment of American ground forces could produce success. In April Johnson authorised the introduction of two army brigades and yet more marines. By mid-June 1965 US forces in Vietnam had reached a total of 82,000, although offensive operations other than the bombing remained limited. Administration arguments about the imperative need to uphold liberty in Asia were not best served when the new South Vietnam Prime Minister, Nguyen Cao Ky, announced that Adolf Hitler was his hero because 'he pulled his country together'.

Through the spring and early summer the pressure on the Johnson administration to adopt a more aggressive strategy increased. The bombing campaign was not bringing the desired results. The Vietnamese forces were reeling before the Viet Cong, the South Vietnam government again seemed on the verge of collapse, and the head of the US military mission in Vietnam, General William Westmoreland, wanted his troops more than doubled so that he might 'take the war to the enemy'. By July Johnson decided that he had little alternative to escalation. A continuation of the existing strategy would bring only a slow defeat, while withdrawal would mean surrender to the communists, with all the fateful consequences this would have for American prestige, the stability of Southeast Asia, and the viability of the Johnson presidency. At the end of the month Johnson cautiously announced that US service personnel would be increased to 125,000, with more to be sent later if needed.

This was not a gung-ho president lightly throwing American might at refractory Asian peasants. Lyndon Johnson was deeply agonised and often depressed during the summer of 1965, not wanting to risk American casualties in Vietnam but unable to accept defeat there. He realised only too well that the United States could be sucked deeper and deeper into the quagmire, which he also knew could wreck his cherished Great Society programmes. One reason for minimising the American commitment publicly at this time was that some of Johnson's reform measures were still before Congress. Lady Bird Johnson later told the president's biographer, Robert Dallek, of her husband's torment over the war: 'It was just a hell of a thorn stuck in his throat. It wouldn't come up; it wouldn't go down. ... It was just pure hell and did not have that reassuring, strong feeling that this is right, that he had when he was in a crunch with civil rights or poverty or education'. Johnson himself once compared his dilemma to that of 'a hitchhiker caught in a hailstorm on a Texas highway': 'I can't run. I can't hide. And I can't make it stop'.

The administration hoped that the intensified force would persuade Hanoi that the Communists could not win the war. By October there were 200,000 US troops in Vietnam. The press and public opinion broadly supported Johnson's policy, insofar as he revealed it. A Gallup Poll in November showed a 64 per cent approval of US involvement in the war, as against 21 per cent opposed. Nonetheless American commitment was growing with little explanation by the White House and little genuine public debate. There were those who distrusted the news management by the administration and Johnson's 'credibility gap' began to show.

Step by step, the American military commitment in Vietnam grew ever larger. The nearly 200,000 US troops there at the end of 1965 grew to 450,000 a year later. Little more than a year again there were 500,000. By early 1968 an estimated 220,000 Viet Cong soldiers had been killed, but it was the body bags being brought home from Vietnam that most distressed the American public. Compared to the number of Vietnamese who died American casualties were relatively light, but they increased remorselessly. By the middle of 1967 nearly 70,000 Americans had been wounded or killed; by the end of 1968 the figure had reached 130,000. (There were ultimately to be about 58,000 American deaths, compared to over two million Vietnamese.) A greater weight of bombs was dropped on Vietnam between July 1965 and December 1967 alone than the Allies dropped on Europe during the entire Second World War. Military expenditure rocketed from $50 billion in 1965 to over $80 billion in 1968. As US commitment and casualties mounted, the White House continued to insist that the United States would not abandon its South Vietnam ally. By the end of 1967 Johnson desperately wanted a peace, but not at the cost of a unilateral American withdrawal. 'I'm not going to be the first American President to lose a war', he told newsman David Brinkley.

At the end of January 1968 the communists launched the Tet offensive. In this massive assault the communists struck not only at Saigon, but also at five of South Vietnam's largest cities and thirty-six of its provincial capitals. Even the US embassy was invaded. Within two months 4,000 American troops and 5,000 South Vietnamese soldiers had died. In fact, US firepower ensured that Tet resulted in defeat for the communists, who lost perhaps 50,000 soldiers. But the relatively large scale of American losses at the hands of an allegedly exhausted enemy did the White House great political harm. The half-a-million American troops in South Vietnam had been unable to protect the country. After an initial patriotic rallying to the president's position, the American public's support for the war dropped. Early in March a public opinion poll showed 49 per cent of respondents saying that sending US troops to fight had been a mistake; 41 per cent supported the policy.

By this time even Secretary of Defense Robert McNamara had despaired of a satisfactory outcome to the war and had been replaced by Clark Clifford. Johnson remained loath to beat a retreat in Vietnam. 'We shall and we are going to win', he declared in March. But a request from the Joint Chiefs for another massive escalation, in the form of a reserve call-up of over 200,000 troops, with half of them to go to Vietnam, shook the White House, which after all had claimed to have won the Tet encounter. Sensitive to the shifting currents of opinion, Clifford seized the opportunity to encourage a change of direction. He arranged a meeting with the 'Wise Men', senior foreign policy experts like Dean Acheson and McGeorge Bundy, who in the past had broadly endorsed Johnson's wishes but who now urged disengagement. 'These establishment bastards have bailed out', a bitter president was reported as saying, although he was probably already reaching a similar conclusion himself. Johnson, whose personal standing had been falling in the polls and who faced raucous anti-war protests, increasing criticism from opinion-makers and an uncertain fight for renomination, could no longer push out of his mind the need for a change of strategy.

At the end of March Johnson went on television to announce a partial bombing halt in North Vietnam and a willingness to enter peace talks. He also announced that, in the interests of achieving peace and reuniting the country, he would not be a candidate for re-election. But the remaining months of his presidency dragged on without disengagement from Vietnam being secured. Johnson sent representatives to preliminary peace talks in Paris in May, and at the end of October announced an end to all bombing of North Vietnam. But the damage inflicted on his party by his policies and by events was already too great, and in November Republican Richard Nixon was elected with vague talk about a 'secret plan' to end the war.

Vietnam was the administration's biggest foreign problem, but it was not the only one, and Johnson was wary of communist encroachments elsewhere too. One area in which it was vital to preserve 'freedom' was Latin America. Kennedy's Alliance for Progress was faltering by 1963, with little achieved in the way either of economic development or democratisation. Johnson came to use it as a vehicle for encouraging private business investment and supporting anticommunist governments. The most serious Latin American problem to confront Johnson concerned the Dominican Republic. In April 1965 an uprising threatened the pro-American regime of the businessman dictator, and Johnson sent in US Marines, ostensibly to protect American lives on the island. But he also evidently feared a Castro-style coup, in a television address in May talking of 'communist leaders' taking 'increasing control' of the rebel forces. Eventually the Organisation of American States sent in a peace-keeping force, including US troops, and a pro-American government was freely elected in 1966. Public opinion generally supported Johnson's policy, although his critics thought that he had exaggerated the communist threat. 'It suddenly occurred to me that maybe they weren't telling the truth in Vietnam either', recalled a Peace Corps official of the invasion of the Dominican Republic. The Dominican 'crisis' made its own contribution to Johnson's emerging 'credibility gap'.

More challenging was the critical situation in the Middle East. In June 1967 the Six Days War broke out between Israel and the Arab states of Egypt, Jordan and Syria. Israeli forces quickly established superiority and took the Sinai, the west bank of the Jordan, east Jerusalem and the Golan Heights. Johnson pressed for a cease-fire, worried that backing Israel (an old US ally) might lead to confrontation with the Soviet Union, which had links with the Arab states. The State Department announced that the United States would be 'neutral in thought, word and deed', to the fury of the Israelis and their influential American supporters. The statement also did little to placate the Arab states, which suspected the United States of aiding the Israelis in any case, and a number of them severed relations with Washington. The Soviet Union threatened to intervene, and the United States eventually prevailed on Israel to agree to a cease-fire. With Israel hanging on to its territorial gains, the position in the Middle East remained tense.

Such regional crises might be more safely handled if the United States could reach a better understanding with the Soviet Union, and Lyndon Johnson looked for ways of easing US-Soviet relations, difficult though that was with his troops in Vietnam. He met the Soviet premier briefly when the latter visited the United States in 1967, and in June 1968 was able to secure one of their mutual diplomatic goals, a Nuclear Nonproliferation Treaty. Some fifty-six countries agreed that nuclear weapons should be limited to the powers possessing them, and the nuclear powers agreed to work for arms control and disarmament. Johnson hoped to maintain the momentum through a visit to Moscow, but in August Soviet troops invaded Czechoslovakia and US-Soviet relations again deteriorated. Johnson left office never having visited the Soviet Union.

The challenges both of securing American withdrawal from Vietnam and improving relations with the communist bloc fell to Johnson's Republican successor, Richard Nixon. The new president, even more than Kennedy, fancied himself an expert on foreign affairs. He made another expert, Henry Kissinger, his National Security Adviser. Nixon came into office with ambitious thoughts of restructuring foreign policy, and had already hinted that the time may have come for the United States to recognise the People's Republic of China. Some kind of easing of relationships with the communist world would be a major coup for a Republican president. But he had also promised 'peace with honor' in Vietnam, and he desperately needed fairly quickly to disentangle the United States from that imbroglio.

That objective was to prove frustratingly elusive. 'Peace with honor' seemed to mean that the United States would somehow have to withdraw from Vietnam without being seen to have surrendered, and this in turn meant the survival of the South Vietnam government. Nixon was no more anxious than Johnson to be the first president to lose a war, and, in the words of Henry Kissinger, 'we could not simply walk away from an enterprise involving two administrations, five allied countries, and thirty-one thousand dead as if we were switching a television channel'. Ultimately Nixon's tactics were to be a variation on Lyndon Johnson's, relying on increased bombing to force the North Vietnamese to the negotiating table and a new diplomatic offensive. The strategy settled on was 'Vietnamisation'. American soldiers were to be progressively withdrawn and the South Vietnam government and forces substantially strengthened, so that Asian boys would once more become the combat troops. A reduction in American casualties, it was hoped, would diminish the anti-war sentiment at home. But Vietnamisation proved disappointingly slow to effect. After a year Nixon had succeeded only in reducing the 550,000 military personnel left by Johnson to 475,000.

The key to peace in Vietnam could lie in the larger world strategy adopted by the United States. Nixon and Kissinger appreciated that global power configurations had been changing, and Nixon, always eager for the 'big play' and looking to his place in history, was anxious to give them a nudge. The United States could no longer dominate world affairs in the manner that it might have hoped after the Second World War. The Soviet economy had been relatively buoyant in the 1960s and the Soviet Union was closing the missile gap. China too was a nuclear power. Elsewhere, the growth of the European Economic Community promised greater political independence for western Europe, Japan had become a major economic power, and new nations had emerged in Africa and Asia. John Kennedy had begun to question bipolar assumptions, and by the Nixon years the need to adapt American foreign policy to multi-polar realities was becoming inescapable.

Nixon remained a Cold Warrior, and international communism continued to be the enemy, but given the constraints on resources and an appreciation of the limits of American might, the way forward seemed to be to establish more stable relationships between the major powers. They in turn could be expected to control their smaller client states, that is to keep order within their own spheres of influence. Co-operation rather than confrontation with the Soviet Union and China would maintain the balance of power and contain aggression. In 1969 the president also announced the Nixon Doctrine, giving notice that in the future the United States would help threatened countries with economic and military aid but would not send combat troops. Détente, as the various theories being developed by Nixon and Kissinger became known in the 1970s, might also facilitate withdrawal from Vietnam.

In 1971 Richard Nixon announced that he would visit the People's Republic of China, the very power that was said to be behind the North Vietnamese (although by this date the latter were growing closer to the Soviet Union). Since 1949 the United States had treated the People's Republic of China as a pariah state, denying it diplomatic recognition and trading relations. Nixon's old anticommunist credentials served him well, protecting him from attacks from the right, while the increasingly acrimonious split between the Soviet Union and China opened an opportunity. In February 1972, as the presidential election campaign was looming, Nixon became the first American president to visit China. The occasion was lavishly covered by the media, and the two sides settled on a series of economic and cultural exchanges. Richard Nixon had won a stunning diplomatic victory, achieving rapprochement with a major enemy. US trade with China was soon booming.

Withdrawing from Vietnam might also require Soviet help, and three months after winning his accord with China Richard Nixon visited Moscow. His objective was détente and a desire to drive a wedge between the two main components of the communist bloc. Again the Republican president secured agreements, telling the Soviet premier Leonid Brezhnev that capitalism and communism could 'live together and work together'. The Soviet Union had its own reasons for seeking better relations, not least its fear of a nuclear China. The meeting was productive. One result was the Strategic Arms Limitation Treaty (SALT), limiting the numbers of offensive intercontinental ballistic missiles maintained by the two powers. Where Kennedy and Johnson had sought nuclear superiority over the Soviet Union, Nixon was prepared to settle for 'sufficiency' or parity. Nixon and Brezhnev also entered pledges to avoid confrontation and to promote economic exchanges, and US-Soviet trade quickly expanded. Richard Nixon returned ready to seek re-election in the presidential contest of 1972 with his reputation as a statesman greatly enhanced.

But communism was to be contained not comforted and it was not to be tolerated just anywhere. When the socialist Salvador Allende sought election as president of Chile in 1970, Nixon, anxious to avert another Cuba, cut off aid to the country and used the CIA to intervene. 'I don't see why we have to let a country go Marxist just because its people are irresponsible', Henry Kissinger is reported to have observed. Allende's election was not averted, but the CIA worked for his overthrow, and this was effected via a military coup in September 1973. Allende died, reportedly committing suicide.

As it happened, the policies of détente proved of little use in disengaging the United States from Vietnam. After two years of 'Vietnamisation' US forces in the country had been reduced only by about half (although as the 1972 election approached the number dropped much faster, and by September was down to 40,000.) The peace negotiations dragged dispiritingly on too, despite massive bombing campaigns launched by the president designed to weaken North Vietnamese resolve. Nixon also took the war into Cambodia, through which the North Vietnamese had been supplying their forces in the south. As early as March 1969 Nixon ordered the secret bombing of sanctuaries used by the North Vietnamese on Cambodian territory, and in April 1970 he announced an invasion of Cambodia by US and South Vietnamese forces. This extension of the war into another country triggered enormous protests in the United States, particularly on the campuses, and at one, Kent State, students were killed when the Ohio National Guard opened fire. Congress finally acted to restrain presidential power, prohibiting the return of American troops to Cambodia. And still the peace process dragged on. Not until January 1973 did Nixon achieve his 'peace with honor', and American forces were withdrawn. Two years later the weak government left in South Vietnam succumbed to the communists.

'The Great Republic has come into its own; it stands first among the peoples of the earth,' the *New York Herald Tribune* had observed as the Second World War was ending, echoing Henry Luce's belief that the 'American Century' had dawned. This vision that it was the destiny of the United States to regulate the global order had sustained successive American administrations in the post-war years. It was one shared by President Kennedy when he had reminded his fellow Americans that the 'hopes of mankind rest upon us'. But these ambitious desires did not survive the 1960s intact. As early as 1966 Senator William Fulbright, chairman of the Senate Foreign Relations Committee, had begun to question the premises of American policy, which he thought betrayed the 'arrogance of power', admonishing American leaders that they were not qualified 'to play God'. By the end of the decade it had become even clearer that the United States did not possess the capacity to manage the course of world events. It was Vietnam in particular which had become the test of American power. Not only was the country achingly divided, but around the globe too former admirers were less responsive to American charms.

Lyndon Johnson himself had writhed at the foreign policy critiques being developed by Fulbright and others, but could not publicly acknowledge their force. Richard Nixon was somewhat freer to seek a new strategy, and his initiatives reflected something of the lessons of the Sixties. The attempts at détente, at reaching accommodation with other major powers, was an admission that the United States could no longer alone act as world guardian. The Nixon Doctrine recognised that American public opinion would not readily accept the expenditure of American lives in foreign fields. Subsequent administrations in their own way sought to come to terms with the limits of American power and the constraints of public opinion. Congress put checks on the capacity of the White House to act independently in foreign policy. Military interventions did take place, but tended either to be severely circumscribed in scope, as in the Reagan administration's invasion of the tiny island of Grenada, or else characterised by overwhelming force, as in the 1990–1 Gulf War. Above all, the American public was to be spared the sight of returning body bags.

The Vietnam War was the only war that the United States palpably lost. Its psychological effects on Americans were profound. It destroyed the post-war consensus on the US role in the world. Something of the divisions were reflected in the post-mortem on what had gone wrong in Vietnam. Some complained that American politicians had been too slow and grudging in providing the military with the weapons needed to win. A massive intervention early enough would have achieved victory, on this analysis, but America's warriors had been 'stabbed in the back' by timorous politicians, an irresponsible press and an unpatriotic anti-war movement. Others believed that the United States should never have intervened, that its Cold War preconceptions and bipolar view of the world had misled it into seeing a threat to its interests where none existed. In any case, the anti-war argument often went, a conventional war against a nationalist movement in the jungles of Southeast Asia was destined to fail. Such views exploded in the press during and after the Vietnam War and have been echoed in various ways in the scholarship.

The erosion of American status in the world, of course, did not begin with Vietnam. The size of the American economy relative to the global economy had been diminishing for many years, and by the late 1960s the country was suffering from serious balance of payments and other economic problems. Nixon's rethinking of American foreign policy was paralleled by changes in international economic and monetary policy. During his administration the dollar's convertibility to gold was ended and the United States in effect ceased to act as the world's banker.

While economic forces had long been quietly chipping away at the foundations of American strength, Vietnam exposed the limits of American power and humiliated the United States as never before. The consequences of the 'Vietnam syndrome' continued to reverberate through American life for the rest of the century. The war had already done something to destroy Lyndon Johnson's cherished Great Society, as it also intensified the inflation that roared through the economy in the 1970s. It added to the perception that governments enjoyed little power to control either domestic or foreign affairs and contributed to the conservative backlash against 'big government'. A part of the reaction against activist government owed something to a heightened distrust of politicians. Lyndon Johnson's misleading statements on Vietnam had opened up a 'credibility gap', as political commentators exposed the falsity of his claims. Richard Nixon's attempts to keep some part of his conduct of the war secret from the public, and the subsequent exposure of his dubious means, added to the low respect in which Americans held their public servants.

Vietnam has sometimes been characterised as the liberals' war. Given the bellicose language of Senator Barry Goldwater during the 1964 presidential campaign and the expansion of the war during the Nixon presidency, it may be doubted whether US commitment would have been any the less had Republicans commanded the White House during most of the 1960s. But it was during the Democratic presidencies of

John Kennedy and especially Lyndon Johnson that fatal decisions were made to escalate the American presence in Southeast Asia, and while the preservation of American prestige may have been critical at each juncture, ostensibly the war was being fought for the ideals Kennedy had articulated in his Inaugural Address. American liberalism was cripplingly compromised by Vietnam. To many on the left, liberalism was exposed as a front for corporate capitalism and imperialism; to some on the right, liberalism had been too weak to uphold American dignity. For Americans of many persuasions, it became more difficult to take a benign view of the nation state.

CHAPTER 5

The Politics of Reaction: From Johnson to Nixon

The hope and optimism of the early 1960s were replaced by darker emotions in the second half of the decade. If nothing else, the horrific murders of public figures told Americans that all was not well with their society. The assassination of John Kennedy in 1963 proved to be but the first of such acts. In February 1965 the African American radical Malcolm X (who had referred to the Kennedy death as a case of 'chickens coming home to roost') was murdered, and in 1967 the leader of the small American Nazi party, George Lincoln Rockwell, was shot to death. In April 1968 Martin Luther King was gunned down, and in June of that year presidential candidate Robert Kennedy was also assassinated. Another presidential candidate, George Wallace, just missed death a few years later when he was shot and left paralysed in May 1972.

Something of the temper of the times might also be gauged by the names of presidential commissions that were set up to study current problems. In July 1967 Lyndon Johnson appointed a Commission on Civil Disorders and a year later he created another body, the National Commission on the Causes and Prevention of Violence. In 1968 too he established the President's Commission on Obscenity and Pornography. In 1970 Richard Nixon was to appoint a Commission on Campus Unrest. These bodies told a different story to that of the President's Commission on Natural Beauty, established by Lyndon Johnson at the height of his authority in 1965. The 'beloved community' of which Martin Luther King had dreamed seemed nowhere in sight.

Disorder and violence assumed a variety of disturbing forms. One way in which the law was flouted was in the burgeoning use of drugs, notably marijuana and LSD. Serious crime figures themselves were rising fast, in contrast to the 1950s, conveying a sense that society was breaking down. The murder rate doubled between 1963 and 1970. The 'long hot summers' of 1965, 1966, and 1967 were punctuated by riots in the urban ghettos, and black violence flared early in 1968 with the assassination of Martin Luther King in April. The Black Panthers began patrolling their territory with guns, and from time to time were involved in fatal shoot-outs with the police. A myriad of lawful protests advertised the degree of public disharmony. Women, Native Americans, students, gays and others marched to demand their rights. Vietnam in particular became the focus of massive dissent. There had been some small protests against American involvement in Vietnam even during the Kennedy administration, but from 1965 as the war escalated so did the demonstrations. Some half-a-million people participated in anti-war demonstrations in New York and San Francisco in April 1967. Young men publicly burned their draft cards, and some went to prison for doing so. Politicians of all stripes called for the restoration of 'law and order' in countless campaign speeches. Turbulence continued until the end of the decade. Angry disturbances erupted on over half the country's campuses in May 1970 after four students were killed at a demonstration at Kent State University in Ohio.

The liberal consensus of the early 1960s, the broad middle ground that the Kennedy and Johnson administrations sought to occupy, was fragmenting. There had been savage assaults on it from both right and left, and by the late 1960s centrist liberals found their political support diminishing fast. The fundamental premises of American public policy were now in question. On the domestic front, it had been broadly accepted since the Second World War that the kinds of social and economic policies associated with the New Deal, in the form of positive government programmes, had been effective and desirable. In foreign affairs, Cold War and containment policies had been endorsed by all mainstream politicians. By the end of the decade the agreement on these issues was disappearing. There was growing resistance to the policies of the Great Society and mounting disillusionment with the American involvement in Vietnam. Criticism of government programmes and criticism of the war emanated (for the most part) from different parts of the political spectrum, but between them they eroded the ground occupied by the centre.

On the right, George Wallace, breaking away from the Democratic party, represented a populist rejection of liberal politics, and he displayed a disturbing popularity not only among some white southerners but also in working and middle class wards in northern cities. As liberals became identified with the establishment, they risked being displaced as allies of the underprivileged by conservatives of the Wallace stripe. Targeting similar constituencies was another conservative, Richard Nixon, seeking to build a new majority for the Republican party. Nonetheless Lyndon Johnson had expected attacks from the right, and much of his strategy, not least over Vietnam, was designed to protect him from angry conservatives. What he was much less prepared for was revolt on the left. Increasingly it was the New Left that was assailing liberalism. These radicals helped to bring an end to the Johnson presidency, but the angry presence of many of them in the Democratic party also disturbed many mainstream voters. The turmoil in the 'vital centre' and on the left were to help Nixon to the White House. He was uniquely placed to exploit both forms of reaction – both against Sixties liberalism and against the war.

Nothing better illustrated the erosion of consensus liberalism than the unexpected eruption of radical protest. The origins of the New Left are usually traced to the creation of the Students for a Democratic Society (SDS) in 1960, and the SDS began to attract national attention in 1965 when it organised the first large demonstration against American policy in Vietnam. A host of other protest groups also came to be associated with the New Left, such as the Student Nonviolent Coordinating Committee and the Youth International Party (Yippies). While the New Left took its vitality largely from opposition to the Vietnam War, other radical movements were also gaining in force and publicity. The civil rights movement was being displaced by the various advocates of Black Power, such as the Black Panthers founded in 1966. In the same year the women's movement took a radical turn with the creation of the National Organization for Women, which by the end of the decade was flanked by yet more radical groups, such as the Women's International Terrorist Conspiracy from Hell (WITCH). If the radical groups displayed a disenchantment with the established order, they also courted reaction from middle America.

Political and social fragmentation were not the only phenomena to worry attentive American analysts. There were signs that the economic good times themselves were coming to an end. From about 1967 productivity was weakening and inflation was rising. The balance of payments situation was worsening, and there was a major gold crisis in the spring of 1968. The real gross income of workers fell in the last two years of the decade. Probably these straws in the wind were not very noticeable to most Americans at the time, but the economic strains could not be ignored indefinitely.

When Lyndon Johnson delivered his Inaugural Address in January 1965, however, these various discontents could not be foreseen. The Great Society, he said, pummelling the air with his fists, 'is the excitement of becoming – always becoming, trying, probing, falling, resting, and trying again – but always trying and always gaining'. Through 1965 the driven president was able to maintain much of this excitement, wheedling, cajoling, and arm-twisting Congress into turning his Great Society proposals into legislation. As we have previously seen, 1965 was the high watermark of Great Society reform, as Congress dramatically reshaped the landscape governed by social legislation. The War on Poverty and other ills was being prosecuted with unabated vigour.

But in 1966 the momentum slowed. Lyndon Johnson was finding that he could not after all wage expensive offensives both at home and abroad, at least not without sustaining political damage. He was fiercely committed to social change domestically and to victory in Vietnam, and temperamentally he found it difficult to retreat from either objective. What ultimately hurt him was the pugnacity with which he pursued both goals, even when it was becoming evident that his policies were eroding his popularity. Johnson's attempt to maintain Great Society reform in the wake of ghetto disturbances, when he seemed to be condoning lawlessness, disenchanted some working and middle class white voters, while his escalation of the frustrating war in Vietnam eventually undermined public confidence in his administration.

But there were still Democratic majorities in Congress, and Johnson managed to win some domestic victories. In 1966 he secured his Department of Transportation and legislation improving vehicle and highway safety, and valuable too were measures to clean rivers and expand other environmental safety safeguards. The campaigns of consumer advocate Ralph Nader and of the emerging environmentalists were beginning to have effect. But these were the most significant legislative achievements of that year. There was Johnson's much-publicised Model Cities programme, but as an urban renewal measure it spread aid too thinly and was to fail to revitalise cities in the way the president had hoped. Some Great Society programmes were already proving problematic by 1966, and Johnson's relationship with Sargent Shriver and the Office of Economic Opportunity was growing strained, in part because of the complaints from influential senators and big city mayors over the local Community Action Programs and the involvement in some of them of black activists. As the Vietnam War escalated, Johnson struggled to keep down the costs of domestic programmes, sometimes coming into conflict with his old reform allies.

The turmoil in the cities also undermined the Johnson presidency. The Watts riot of August 1965, with its thirty-four deaths, was much the worst race riot since Detroit in 1943, and its public impact was profound. Northern whites could no longer think of race relations as a southern problem. Press secretary George Reedy observed to the president that there was a risk that 'the rioters will become identified with the civil rights movement and thereby compound the difficulties of those seeking long-range solutions in the U.S.'. After an initial retreat into agonised disbelief, Johnson showed some sympathy for the rioters, warning that the same could occur anywhere where people 'feel they don't get a fair shake'. Where some whites were reacting by demanding welfare cuts and stronger policing, Johnson was reacting by advocating more Great Society reform, exposing himself to the charge that he was rewarding violence. More ghetto disturbances occurred the following year. 'The domestic events of 1966 made it appear that domestic turmoil had become part of the American scene', noted the commission established to examine social disorder. By late that summer a Gallup Poll showed 44 per cent as 'unfavorable' to the Great Society, against 32 per cent 'favorable'.

Something of a reaction against the Great Society could also be discerned in the mid-term elections of 1966, although moderate Republicans tended to fare better than their right-wing associates. That would have given the president little comfort – a moderate Republican candidate for president in 1968 would pose a greater threat to him than another of the Goldwater variety. When Johnson presented his State of the Union Message in January 1967 he maintained the reform rhetoric, but the caution in his words led some to suspect that he now had little heart for further expanding Great Society programmes.

A few days after the mid-term elections the Budget Director reported his worries to the president:

'The problem is simply that *we are not able to fund adequately the new Great Society programs*. At the same time, states, cities, depressed areas and individuals have been led to expect immediate delivery of benefits from Great Society programs to a degree that is not realistic. ... If this goes on long enough, and we do not make good, the Administration loses credibility.'

Disturbed by the demands on the budget, Johnson did call for a 6 per cent tax surcharge. But his loss of standing in the opinion polls meant that the president could no longer bend Congress to his will. By the summer of 1967 inflation was picking up, while the predictions for the budget deficit for fiscal 1968 were reaching a worrying $29 billion. In August Johnson publicly laid out the need for economies and proposed a temporary 10 per cent surcharge on corporate and personal taxes. The draining cost of the war was becoming inescapable.

Such evidence of what could be interpreted as economic mismanagement did Johnson's standing no good; that month his approval rating fell to 39 per cent and the disapproval rating rose to 47 per cent. The public was unconvinced over the tax hike and Congress proved recalcitrant. In theory, an alternative was a major cut in government expenditure, and since defence spending could hardly be curbed in the midst of war, conservatives scented an opportunity to savage the Great Society programmes. Some liberals were also tempted into an unholy alliance with the conservatives: if they resisted the tax surcharge, Johnson might just abandon Vietnam before he abandoned his cherished Great Society. Johnson, however, was loath to abandon either. Former friends doubted whether Johnson could sustain both the War on Poverty and the war in Vietnam. 'Each war feeds on the other', remarked Senator William Fulbright, 'and, although the President assures us that we have the resources to win both wars, in fact we are not winning either of them'.

The continued racial tensions exacerbated Johnson's problems. The ghettos flared up yet again in the summer of 1967, most agonisingly in Newark in June and in Detroit in July, at the respective costs of twenty-three and forty-three deaths. Scenes of civil war were suggested by news pictures of burning buildings, widespread looting and tanks in the streets. Between May and August eight 'major disorders' (requiring the use of federal forces) and thirty-one 'serious disorders' (dealt with by state police) were recorded, mainly in cities of 250,000 or over. After Detroit the Republican party leaders issued a statement saying that 'We are rapidly approaching a state of anarchy and the President has totally failed to recognise the problem'. Johnson almost despaired. He felt – with some justification – that he had done more for African Americans than any previous president, and while he recognised the continued deprivation in the black communities, he could not see how he could offer them any more. Indeed, what he was already providing was being jeopardised by the disturbances.

The urban unrest had also drawn attention to the crime figures. Crime – as opposed to ghetto riots – had become a major issue in its own right. The rising crime rate had been a political football in the mid-term elections of 1966, and was rendered all the more emotive by Supreme Court decisions that seemed to protect the criminal. By January 1967 Johnson felt himself obliged to respond. He proposed a Safe Streets and Crime Control Act, offering federal grants to state and local governments to improve their police systems, and he later asked for a gun control law, though wrangles in Congress frustrated the enactment of these measures. Anxious not to be outflanked by conservatives on the issue, Johnson returned to the fray in 1968: 'There is no more urgent business before this Congress than to pass the Safe Streets Act this year'. In the wake of Robert Kennedy's assassination Congress did enact crime and gun control laws, albeit with mutilating amendments. The real significance of the crime control measure was the extension of federal influence into yet another area; hitherto police matters had been the jealous preserve of state and local governments.

The unprecedented record of deaths and destruction in the ghettos in the summer of 1967 appalled the administration, but the embattled president still struggled for solutions. Suspecting that the ghetto tensions might have more to do with miserable living conditions than lack of jobs, Johnson urged Congress to look to measures to improve housing. He sent another signal to black Americans when he nominated Thurgood Marshall to the Supreme Court. At a time when spiralling crime rates and black unrest were dominating the headlines, and when a white backlash was growing, Lyndon Johnson was placing the first African American on the country's highest court. (Explaining to an aide why he appointed the well-known Marshall rather than a more obscure and less controversial black judge, Johnson said: 'When I appoint a nigger to the bench, I want everyone to know he's a nigger'.)

Johnson boasted that the appointment would lose him votes, and it did nothing to arrest his serious slippage in the polls. An increase to record levels of the number of US troops in Vietnam, the call for the 10 per cent tax surcharge, and the destructive race riots, all concentrated in the summer of 1967, did Johnson's administration irreparable harm. (Meanwhile, in San Francisco, hippies were celebrating the 'Summer of Love'.) A Johnson approval rating of 52 per cent in June had slumped to 38 per cent by October, while the disapproval rating had jumped from 35 to 50 per cent.

The pressure never let up. Opposition to the war was growing both in Congress and in the country at large in the second half of 1967. Administration claims that the United States would prevail were being contradicted by reports in the press. 'Victory is not close at hand', concluded an authoritative account in the *New York Times* in August: 'It may be beyond reach'. By this time prominent figures like Senator Robert Kennedy were regularly criticising government policy. A Gallup Poll in early October showed 57 per cent disapproving and only 28 per cent approving Johnson's 'handling of the war'. Later that month nearly 100,000 people descended on Washington in a two-day peace rally, demonstrating that middle-class liberals were joining student radicals in anti-war protests. Even Johnson's right-hand man, Secretary of Defense McNamara, could no longer go along with administration policy, and in November it was reported that he was leaving office to become head of the World Bank. But the agonised and exasperated president was still in no mood to retreat from Vietnam. In a private meeting with reporters who asked him why the United States was in Vietnam, Johnson, according to his friend Arthur Goldberg, 'unzipped his fly, drew out his substantial organ, and declared, "This is why!".'

By the end of 1967 Johnson was forced not simply to contain domestic spending but also to take the knife to existing Great Society programmes. In December he accepted a reduced appropriation for the Office of Economic Opportunity, and other agencies too suffered substantial cuts. Another casualty was the space programme. Funding for the moon shot was maintained, but NASA found its other programmes being curbed and its director resigned in protest. In space exploration as in other areas of American life, among the public and in government, the optimism and enthusiasm of the early 1960s had given way to wearier emotions. Adding to Johnson's problems in formulating a budget for 1968 was the deteriorating balance of payments deficit and a run on the country's gold reserves. Nonetheless public opinion was still strongly against a tax hike, although Johnson repeated his request for a 10 per cent surcharge.

Johnson was now searching for ways of sustaining the Great Society without much new federal spending. In 1968 he proposed a civil rights initiative to end discrimination in the sale and renting of housing. Quite apart from improving living conditions, integrated housing could lead to better education and job opportunities for African Americans. Such 'open housing' measures were not particularly popular with whites who were uneasy at the prospect of blacks moving into their neighbourhoods, and a similar proposal had foundered on such concerns in 1966, but Johnson pressed the issue. It met opposition in the house of representatives, but the assassination of Martin Luther King in April triggered its passage. Within a week of King's death the Fair Housing measure had become law, a tribute to the slain leader.

With the cost of the war in Vietnam continuing to push up in the wake of the Tet offensive, and Johnson determined to maintain pressure on Hanoi to force the North Vietnamese to the negotiating table, the president needed his tax increase more than ever. The urban riots following King's death also reinforced his reluctance for cuts in domestic programmes. Johnson warned congressional leaders of the risks of major national and international financial crises, and eventually in June a tax bill was agreed. Congress consented to the 10 per cent tax surcharge.

Despite the budget constraints, the indefatigable Johnson continued to prod Congress for reform legislation. Once he had decided not to run for re-election, he became more determined than ever to win new laws. In his last summer and autumn he secured laws to further urban programmes, to aid the handicapped, to train health professionals, to enhance safety standards, to expand consumer protection, and to extend the food stamp programme. While some of these measures involved federal spending, others did not. Containing the deficit remained a priority. Regulating industry, that is imposing minimum standards on all businesses (such as over workers' safety) was one way of carrying reform forward at little cost to the federal government. The network of regulations that business was to complain of in the 1980s were to a significant degree a heritage of the Great Society, as well as of the consumer safety and environmentalist campaigns that gathered strength in these years.

The political damage sustained by New Deal liberalism during the Great Society years was revealed by Johnson's shock decision not to seek re-election. By the end of 1967 he seems seriously to have been considering retiring. The remorseless erosion of his popularity raised doubts as to whether he could win again. Given the dissatisfaction within the party, particularly on its liberal wing, Johnson knew also that he could face competition for the Democratic nomination, and there was speculation in particular that Robert Kennedy would declare himself a candidate. With the Tet offensive at the end of January 1968 Johnson's political standing weakened yet further, and it did nothing too for the physical health of a man who had once had a heart attack.

A rival for the Democratic nomination had in fact emerged in the liberal form of Senator Eugene McCarthy of Minnesota. McCarthy had announced his candidacy in December, promised disaffected youth an 'entrance back into the political process', and sought to mobilise a variety of dissident groups behind an anti-war banner. Congressman Don Edwards spoke for some of McCarthy's supporters when he remembered 1963 as 'the year of hope', a hope brutally betrayed by the president who had taken the country into 'the wicked war in Vietnam'. McCarthy's campaign gathered pace slowly, but he came a disturbingly close second to Johnson in the New Hampshire primary in March with 42 per cent of the vote. Soon after Robert Kennedy announced his own candidacy. By this time Johnson's approval rating had fallen to 36 per cent and disapproval had risen to 52 per cent, and close to two thirds of those polled disliked his policy on Vietnam. At the end of March he withdraw from the campaign.

When the Democratic convention met in August in the ugly atmosphere of Chicago, Johnson made sure not only that the nomination went to his vice-president, Hubert Humphrey, a life-long liberal, but also that the platform endorsed administration policy on Vietnam. The sour scenes projected by the television cameras remained imprinted on the voters' minds. 'The whole world is watching', jeered protesters as the police swung their clubs, although an opinion poll the next month showed 56 per cent supporting the police actions. Republican candidate Richard Nixon was eager to exploit Democratic disarray. He remained vague on domestic matters, and the central issue in the campaign became who was best able to free the United States from Vietnam. So far the administration's efforts had proved in vain, while Nixon gave the voters a shred of hope by implying that he had a 'secret plan' to end the war. This at least seemed to offer diplomatic action in contrast to the Democrats' dispiriting dependency on military might. Lyndon Johnson finally announced a bombing halt on 31 October, in the hope of imparting energy to peace talks in Paris, but Nixon won the popular vote by the same kind of hairbreadth that Kennedy had in 1960.

The election of Richard Nixon owed more to disenchantment with the Johnson administration than it did to his own personal appeal. While the liberal consensus for which Lyndon Johnson had yearned had been fractured, the return of the Republican to the White House was not a triumph for the far right. Nixon appreciated that forging a majority meant winning votes from the centre as well as the right, and he projected himself as a moderate conservative.

Yet there were conservative implications in Nixon's stance, and these were to become more evident as his administration unfolded. The 1968 campaign witnessed the first sighting of his 'southern strategy', as he grasped the potential for further Republican inroads into the traditionally Democratic South. An important tactic was the selection of Spiro Agnew, the Governor of Maryland, as his running-mate. As a resident of a border state Agnew should be acceptable to conservative southerners, but important too was his image as a strong 'law-and-order' figure following his denunciation of urban rioters. Some disenchanted Democrats in the North might even be drawn to him. In order to capitalise on the anti-Johnson sentiment Nixon kept his campaign short on specifics – there was no point in antagonising voters already deserting the Democrats – and his speeches were largely confined to bland rhetoric or to savaging the administration. His scorning of the Great Society's 'knee-jerk reaction of government program' poised him against big government. A believer in the Protestant work ethic, Nixon insisted that his priority was to provide jobs rather than welfare. Further, while he deprecated Wallace's demagoguery, he refused to make overtures to African Americans. 'I'm not going to campaign for the black vote at the risk of alienating the suburban vote,' he told a friend. He largely succeeded – as noted in Chapter 2, he easily led Humphrey in the once-Democratic South and made more modest gains in northern suburbs.

Nixon's decision to pin his hopes on the 'white backlash' was also illustrated by his rhetorical appeal to the 'forgotten Americans', the law-abiding taxpayers 'who had not been shouting and demonstrating'. He had positioned himself not only against the Johnson administration but also against the various protest movements associated with the New Left. White workers need not have been racist to wonder just what the Great Society was offering them, and to question whether their tax dollars should go to ghetto rioters and unruly students. Nixon's victory, it has been said, was a victory for the 'the unyoung, the unblack, and the unpoor'. Whatever his claims to be a moderate, Nixon's broad electoral strategy served to encourage conservative impulses. 'We have endured a long night of the American spirit', he said in his Inaugural Address, turning his back on the Sixties.

Richard Nixon's gracelessness had served him badly in his presidential contest with John Kennedy in 1960, but the two had more in common than was often recognised. Both were intelligent and politically shrewd. Neither possessed a highly articulated political philosophy and their policy positions as presidential candidates remained somewhat vague. Both were essentially pragmatic, and while Kennedy's pragmatism leaned to the liberal end of the political spectrum and Nixon's to the conservative, there was much common ground. Both thought the presidency could be an instrument of change, and there were similarities of temperament in their approach to government. Where Kennedy wanted to be 'tough', Nixon boasted that he thrived on 'crisis'. Where Kennedy believed in an 'active' executive, Nixon was drawn to the 'big play' and held that the mark of a leader was to 'give history a nudge'. Ideological consistency was to be expected from neither.

So it proved with the Nixon administration. Fascinated by the concept of leadership but with a conservative's disdain for 'big' government, Nixon simultaneously sought ways of centralising administrative control in the presidency and of redistributing some services to the states. He wanted to reduce the power of the federal bureaucracy while enhancing that of the White House. This impulse could lead him to stretch the law and the Constitution.

In August 1969 he unveiled the so-called New Federalism, aimed at reducing Washington bureaucracy and congressional interference. One intent was to return federal revenue to the states so that some programmes, particularly the provision of services like education and health, could be managed locally. Congressional committees obstructed proposals which would reduce their own authority, but a revenue-sharing bill eventually became law in 1972. Not all areas of public policy, however, were readily susceptible to decentralisation, among them environmental and energy matters, and these Nixon hoped to make subject to executive rather than congressional direction. Prudently aligning himself with the environmental cause, which had growing support in Congress, Nixon signed legislation establishing the Environmental

Protection Agency in 1970. The promulgation of guidelines from Washington was continuing even under a Republican president.

One area Nixon believed to be a federal responsibility was welfare, although again his vision was born of rather conservative instincts. 'Poverty must be conquered without sacrificing the will to work', he said, 'for if we take the route of the permanent handout, the American character will itself be impoverished'. These were pretty traditional sentiments, though the president's solution was not, for among other things it illustrated his desire to circumvent the federal bureaucracy. Lyndon Johnson had hoped that his War on Poverty would put an end to welfare payments, but the number of Americans on public assistance had jumped from 7.8 million in 1965 to 11.1 million in 1969. One reason for the growth in welfare rolls was the huge movement of poor and mainly rural southern blacks to the northern cities. Another was the greater awareness of poor people of their entitlements and a greater willingness to claim them. The activism of the Sixties characterised many of the poor as well as other groups.

Nixon's Family Assistance Plan (FAP) would provide every American family with a guaranteed annual income ($1,600 for a family of four). Strikingly, people in employment as well as those on welfare would be eligible, so that 'those who work would no longer be discriminated against'; recipients would also be obliged to undertake work or training. The novel approach here was that of a negative income tax. Some liberals liked the idea of a guaranteed income, while certain kinds of conservatives applauded the prospect of sweeping away the welfare bureaucracy while also increasing work incentives. But many Americans were suspicious of what looked like giving benefits as a matter of right. Presidential aide Charles Colson thought that even organised labour was opposed to FAP, which could be 'counterproductive politically to our efforts with the average middle-class working man and the labor movement'. The measure foundered in Congress. Ironically, with its failure Nixon endorsed the introduction nationally of uniform standards in the food stamp programme and automatic cost-of-living increases in social security payments, and these and other adjustments to welfare measures meant that spending on domestic programmes continued to spiral during his administration.

Nixon's belief in the work ethic was also reflected in his claim that the provision of jobs offered the most constructive route to racial equality. Thus his Minority Business Enterprise programme, launched in 1969, provided loans to help African Americans and other minorities to establish small businesses. Similarly the Philadelphia Plan, developed for the construction industry in 1969 and later extended to others, required unions working on federal contracts to admit a quota of African American apprentices to full union membership. Hence originated 'affirmative action' as governmental policy. One motive was to disrupt white-black relations in the labour movement and thus weaken the Democratic party. When the Democrats eventually decided to champion the idea of affirmative action themselves, Nixon tried to extract political advantage by turning against it.

As his retreat from affirmative action indicated, Nixon was never a very convincing champion of racial equality. His need to fend off George Wallace (still chasing presidential hopes) and to build on Republican gains in the South meant that his attitude towards civil rights was at best ambiguous. 'The time may have come when the issue of race could benefit from a period of benign neglect', wrote Pat Moynihan in a White House memo. The new Republican Justice Department permitted delays in school desegregation, although when the Supreme Court in October 1969 insisted that integration must proceed 'at once', the administration resolved to work with the courts rather than risk a constitutional crisis. Desegregation in the South proceeded remarkably rapidly as the administration worked quietly with local leaders to bring school districts into line with the law. The proportion of black children going to segregated schools in the South dropped markedly from 68 per cent in 1968 to 8 per cent in 1972. Some of the credit for this fairly peaceable transition went to white southerners who had come to appreciate that a reputation for racial intransigence was harming the South.

But the use of bussing in order to integrate schools had flared into a contentious issue, and its legality was upheld by the Supreme Court in April 1971. Nixon, worried about George Wallace's popularity in the South, now proved less respectful of the Court. In August he aligned himself with public opinion by signalling his hostility to bussing. After Wallace won the Florida primary in March 1972 with a campaign focusing on the issue, Nixon took to television to call for a 'moratorium' on court-ordered bussing and for legislation to restrict it. Here was a president coming close to inciting people to disobey the law of the land.

Reflective too of Nixon's southern strategy were his Supreme Court appointments. In 1969 he tried to fill a vacancy with a South Carolinian,

Clement F. Haynsworth, Jr. But Haynsworth's record revealed some anti-civil rights and anti-labour positions, and powerful opposition to him soon emerged among Democrats, still in a majority on the senate that would have to confirm the nomination. Despite warnings, the president persisted with Haynsworth, whom the senate eventually rejected. Nixon then nominated G. Harrold Carswell, a Florida judge, but his record proved to be even more in sympathy with white supremacy and his nomination too was lost. A furious Nixon denounced the senate as biased against men who were 'born in the South'. Eventually the slot was filled by the respected conservative Harry Blackmun of Minnesota. But as it happened Nixon was to have a major impact on the Court's composition, even if he was unsuccessful in an attempt to secure impeachment proceedings against its most liberal member, William O. Douglas. In Warren Burger, a moderate conservative, he had already chosen a new Chief Justice to replace Earl Warren, and in 1971 he named two more justices, a conservative southerner Lewis Powell and William Rehnquist, an able strict constructionist who was eventually to become Chief Justice. Lyndon Johnson had hoped for a Supreme Court that would uphold his reform programmes, but Nixon's four appointments made the bench more conservative. While it did not go to war on Great Society laws, it backed away from the activism associated with the Warren Court. Nixon had nudged the governance of the United States towards the right.

Nixon's pragmatism as a conservative, however, was highlighted by his celebrated 'turn-around' on economic policy, one that he dramatised as a major initiative in a television address. The deteriorating balance of payments combined with inflation had contributed to a critical drain on the country's gold reserves. Foreigners were selling dollars on a massive scale, and by the summer of 1971 the economy seemed on the verge of collapse. In August the administration 'closed the gold window' by suspending the convertibility of the dollar into gold. It also introduced its New Economic Policy by imposing a temporary surcharge of 10 per cent on imports. 'My basic approach', said Secretary of the Treasury John Connally, 'is that the foreigners are out to screw us. Our job is to screw them first'. Even more striking perhaps was a ninety-day freeze on prices and wages to control inflation. Wage and price controls were normally anathema to economic conservatives, and they revealed the extent of Nixon's alarm about global and domestic economic pressures. But there were political reasons for the controls too. They were designed to keep down prices as the president sought re-election.

For the most part, however, electoral calculations pointed to a conservative strategy, and nothing better illustrated Nixon's exploitation of the politics of reaction than his administration's treatment of the radical left. In 1969 it levelled conspiracy charges at New Left leaders arrested the previous summer during the disturbances at the Democratic National Convention, the so-called the 'Chicago Eight', including Tom Hayden, Abbie Hoffman, Jerry Rubin, and (in a separate proceeding) Bobby Seale of the Black Panthers. Five of them were convicted after an extraordinary and boisterous trial in which the judge seemed intent on a guilty verdict. (Eventually their convictions were overturned on appeal.) Also at the receiving end of governmental attention were the Black Panthers, who were ruthlessly targeted by the FBI and several police forces. During 1969 their offices were frequently raided, and several Panthers were arrested. In December the American Civil Liberties Union concluded that the 'record of police actions across the country against the Black Panther Party forms a prima facie case ... that law enforcement officials are waging a drive against the black militant organization resulting in serious civil liberties violations'. By the spring of 1970 at least thirty-eight Panthers had died in police shoot-outs and other incidents (one of them while sleeping in his home).

Other protesters too experienced the hostility of the Nixon administration. When a massive anti-war demonstration was organised in Washington in November 1969, 9,000 federal troops were moved in and the Deputy Attorney General muttered: 'We just can't wait to beat up those motherfucking kids'. During a protest at Berkeley in 1969 in which an onlooker died from police buckshot, Governor Ronald Reagan said: 'If it's a blood bath they want, let it be now'. More angry student demonstrations erupted after the revelation in April 1970 that the administration had extended the war into Cambodia, and Nixon railed against 'these bums, you know, blowin' up the campuses'. It was during these demonstrations that four students at Kent State University were shot to death by national guardsmen, and in the subsequent student fury two more died from police bullets at Jackson State College in Mississippi. Whatever the responsibility of local officers for these tragedies, the rhetoric of the Nixon administration had done nothing to restrain the agents of the law.

But the administration's 'law-and-order' stand served it well politically. According to opinion polls taken in the autumn of 1969, over 80 per cent of white Americans believed that campus demonstrators and black militants had been treated 'too leniently'. Polls taken after the Cambodia invasion indicated that around 75 per cent of Americans disapproved of anti-government protests. During the mid-term election campaign of 1970 Vice President Spiro Agnew blamed campus protesters for fomenting violence and insisted that it was 'time to sweep that kind of garbage out of our society'. FBI and Army surveillance of protest groups was stepped up, and when 30,000 peace activists camped out in Washington in May 1971, police and armed soldiers arrested a record 12,000. In 1972 Richard Nixon was well placed to run against what survived of the New Left.

Despite – though in significant part because of – the public demonstrations that punctuated Nixon's first term, there was little doubt that he would be re-elected. His foreign policy coups in Peking and Moscow overshadowed the failure to end the war in Vietnam, which became a somewhat less contentious issue as the number of US troops there was scaled back. Further, the course of domestic politics was turning to Nixon's advantage, particularly when the Democratic party nominated George McGovern for president. It was clear that the 'new politics' associated with the Democratic left held little appeal for what Nixon called 'the silent majority', and he again sought to occupy the centre and this time won with a landslide (see Chapter 2). The voters were repudiating not so much the Democratic party (which retained its majorities in Congress) but the radical political styles that had emerged from the 1960s. The misfortune of the McGovern campaign was its association with the long-haired lifestyle of the counter-culture. Keen to get out of Vietnam and prepared to extend amnesty to draft dodgers, George McGovern's position could be ridiculed as 'acid, amnesty, and abortion'. Richard Nixon may not have been a doctrinaire conservative, but he was at one with the 'silent majority' in upholding tradition on social order and lifestyle issues and in discountenancing surrender in Vietnam.

Assisting him win the election, however, were the burglars who had broken into the offices of the Democratic National Committee in the Watergate complex in Washington. Their arrests at first attracted little attention, but the Watergate issue was to unravel fatally over the next two years and in August 1974 bring down the Nixon presidency. Among the agents of Nixon's downfall was Judge John J. Sirica, whose appointment to the federal bench Nixon had approved because of his reputation as a champion of 'law-and-order'.

The Nixon administration marked the ending of the Sixties. 'Above all', Arthur Schlesinger had written at the outset of the decade, 'there will be a sense of motion, of leadership, and of hope'. Those characteristics did seem to be present for a time, but hope had eventually given way to cynicism. Richard Nixon's election was made possible by the crumbling of the New Deal Order, by disillusion with New Frontier and Great Society liberalism, and by the sorry Johnson record in Vietnam. His re-election represented a repudiation of street politics.

Nixon himself itched to exercise executive leadership, but he had disavowed the 'big government' philosophy of the Democrats, while the adoption of a stance of 'benign neglect' with respect to civil rights contrasted with the activism of the Kennedy and Johnson administrations. The Nixon Doctrine signalled a break with the policy that had led to the extensive deployment of combat troops in Vietnam. He appreciated the need to retain the support of the political centre, but his electoral posture served to encourage those currents that were reacting against Sixties liberalism. His cautious 'southern strategy' made him beholden to white backlash voters who were displaying conservative attitudes on a range of racial and lifestyle issues. His appointments to the Supreme Court edged it away from the judicial activism of the Warren Court. His campaigns against black radicals and rebellious students tapped the sentiments of the 'silent majority'. The political and cultural conservatism of the Nixon administration were to ease the way for the rise of the New Right.

PART 3

Popular Protest and New Movements

When he took the presidential oath of office John Kennedy had issued Americans with a challenge: 'ask not what your country can do for you – ask what you can do for your country'. Earlier, in accepting the Democratic nomination, he had given some indication of the issues that self-sacrificing Americans might address – 'peace and war', 'ignorance and prejudice', 'poverty and surplus'. He could hardly have anticipated that so many of his fellow citizens would take him at his word.

The protest movements of the 1960s were the product of a complex convergence of circumstances. Demographic change was one source, as African Americans exchanged rural for urban environments and as the proportion of young people in the population increased fast. The processes associated with post-industrialism multiplied the numbers in universities, brought more women into the labour force, and expanded the 'new class' of professional workers whose interests were not necessarily tied to either capital or labour. Prosperity was another influence, suggesting that there were ample resources for everyone and underlining the disparity between the 'haves' and the 'have nots'. Even some of the more financially secure Americans were disaffected by the material comfort that surrounded them, unable to reconcile the disparities in privilege with American ideals. Steady economic growth also served for a time to vindicate the conventional wisdom of the day, which valued the guidance of experts and the benign potential of government. Such assumptions not only promoted a more activist spirit in Washington, but also in the country at large, as groups mobilised to secure their preferred policies – which is also to say access to resources. Martin Luther King Jr was one of those who believed that government could make a difference. Public policies were often less the product of initiatives from Washington and more responses to pressures from below.

Inevitably there was disaffection and disappointment. Some young people were alienated by the powerlessness they felt in an increasingly bureaucratic post-industrial order. In the moderate early years of the New Left, civil rights and women's movements, there were many who hoped to work with the liberals in government and in the courts, but the demands for inclusion placed great strains on the political system. Groups claiming rights as a matter of principle often saw compromise as a form of surrender, and the expectations heightened both by the momentum of a movement and by governmental promises could not always be met. Some citizens took to the streets in disillusionment, turning to radicalism and revolution rather than to reform. In any case, the liberationist spirit of the Sixties sent many Americans, particularly among the young, into quests to rebuild their own communities or to seek personal fulfilment. The extraordinary revolt of African Americans raised the consciousness of other groups, in turn spurring an interest in identity politics that was to call into question the cohesion of the social order. If conservatives were ultimately largely successful in the conventional arena of national party politics, they were often helpless to arrest the processes of social and cultural change.

CHAPTER 6

The African American Revolt: From Civil Rights to Black Power

No Americans were more committed to the Sixties' belief in the efficacy of action than those of African descent. The countless students who sat in at lunch counters demanding to be served, the black preachers who led marches calling for integration, the Black Panthers who patrolled the ghettos with guns, the cultural nationalists who adopted African names – all were taking forms of action to assert their identity and claim their rights. Black air force veteran James Meredith presented himself at the all-white University of Mississippi in September 1962 and demanded to be admitted; Muhammad Ali in April 1967 refused to be drafted into the armed forces, saying that he did not wish to fight for white America; in 1968, at the Mexican Olympics, athletes Tommie Smith and John Carlos gave the Black Power salute as they were receiving their medals. Innumerable acts, individual and collective, gave expression to the extraordinary assertiveness of African Americans in these years. Perhaps some were existential acts, designed to give meaning to the life of the actor; others were designed to produce a response or to promote a climate in which reform was possible. Black activism, whether spontaneous or organised, served both to instil pride among African Americans and to effect change.

Black protest also had a profound moral effect on American society. Many white Americans did not respond favourably to it, but others did. White liberalism in the 1960s espoused a humanitarian ethic and betrayed guilt at the historic treatment of racial minorities in the United States. As John Kennedy put it in 1963, it was simply unacceptable for a people committed to freedom to say that 'we have no second-class citizens except Negroes'. But the civil rights movement did much more than simply touch the conscience of white citizens. It also raised the consciousness of many ethnic groups. Mexican Americans held their

First Chicano National Conference in 1969; Asian Americans, Native Americans and others were similarly emboldened to assert their identities and claim their rights. It was the civil rights movement, assisted by the Supreme Court, not the presidential administrations, which performed the vital work of educating the public on the meaning of rights.

The dawn of the new decade indeed witnessed an extraordinary explosion of black protest across the South. The year 1960 saw the widespread use of the sit-in tactic. One Monday in February four well-dressed black students sat down at the whites-only lunch counter in a Woolworth store in Greensboro, North Carolina, and politely asked to be served. They were ignored but they persisted and in the following days other black and some white students joined them. By Thursday over a hundred students awaited service; by Friday there were a thousand. When the students were arrested, Greensboro blacks organised a massive boycott of other stores in the town, and, faced by plummeting profits and embarrassing publicity, the business community gave in and the stores were integrated.

Buoyed by media publicity, sit-ins at lunch counters, shopping centres, restaurants and theatres took place throughout the South, even in the Deep South. By September 1961 it was estimated that over 800 sit-ins had occurred, involving perhaps some 70,000 people of all races, of whom 4,000 were arrested. From out of this stunning activity there emerged the Student Nonviolent Coordinating Committee (SNCC), formed in 1960 by militant young blacks. Like other Sixties leftist organisations, SNCC saw itself as a loose federation of largely autonomous local groups. Another product of the ferment was the revival of an old black spiritual, emerging in its modern form as 'We Shall Overcome'.

These sit-ins were not led by the established civil rights organisations. To a large extent they represented the spontaneous action of southern black youth, growing impatient with the cautious ways of their elders. The participants were young blacks who had for the most part been able to get to college and who had experience of urban life. Well-educated and aware of the course of public events, they had come to maturity as black leaders like Martin Luther King were beginning to be heard. Their anger that African Americans were being widely denied their constitutional rights was sharpened by frustration at the obstacles in the paths of their own careers – they could not easily go on to graduate school or into the higher professions like their white contemporaries.

And, while they risked beatings and jail, in many cases they did not have jobs to lose or families to support. They were uniquely placed to express the moral anger of black America. And their sophistication and neat dress made the point that blacks were not necessarily best suited to being janitors and dirt farmers.

The demographic and socioeconomic changes in the circumstances of American blacks since the 1940s had been creating conditions more conducive to protest activity. As blacks moved into cities, in the South as elsewhere, they sometimes had access to better (if still segregated) educational facilities, more varied job opportunities and more favourable conditions for organisation. When southern states moved to pre-empt the Supreme Court by spending more on the black school systems to sustain the pretence that they really were equal, they were helping to create better-educated high school graduates. Some went on to black colleges. By 1950 some 4.5 per cent of blacks of college age were in higher education, far short of the white per centage but not far off the figure for British youth (5.8 per cent in 1954). In 1940 only 1.6 per cent of non-whites had had four years of college; by 1960 the figure had jumped to 5.4 per cent. The per centage of blacks in professional and white-collar occupations was also rising. Some black graduates joined the ministry, and African American church culture was to provide a rich spiritual and financial base for the civil rights movement. These various sociological trends were occurring at the same time as geopolitical conditions were evolving in ways favourable to the African American cause. A narrow presidential election could turn on the growing black vote in northern cities. The advent of the Cold War and the self-appointment of the United States as the champion of the 'free world' meant that the visible presence of second-class citizens was highly embarrassing to American leaders. Further, the success of nationalist movements in Africa in throwing off European rule was not lost on black Americans.

From time-to-time in the 1950s local groups of blacks succeeded in mobilising in protest against particular conditions in southern cities. In 1955–6, a boycott in Montgomery, Alabama, won widespread attention. In December 1955 black seamstress Rosa Parks sat down in the white section of a Montgomery bus and was promptly arrested. Local blacks mobilised on her behalf, organised a boycott of the city's buses, and persuaded a young Baptist minister, Martin Luther King Jr, to act as their leader. Local blacks also challenged bus segregation in the courts, and in November 1956 the Supreme Court declared it unconstitutional. Just before Christmas, Martin Luther King and his black and white friends rode together at the front of a Montgomery bus.

The Montgomery boycott had focused attention on the technique of non-violent protest. Direct action held some potential for African Americans, representing an alternative to the slow-moving reliance on the judicial process favoured by the National Association for the Advancement of Colored People (NAACP). The massive resistance to integration practised by the racist white South seemed to demand a determined response, and peaceful direct action was a strategy which allowed ordinary blacks to play a part. Martin Luther King was much impressed by Gandhi's use of non-violent protest against British rule in India, and his own upbringing and theological study instilled in him a commitment to social justice. Christian love and forgiveness, not hate, were to be displayed towards the oppressor. The philosophy of non-violent protest, drawing as it did on Christian traditions, touched a chord in many southern blacks. In 1957 King and other black ministers organised the Southern Christian Leadership Conference (SCLC), and King himself was soon travelling and speaking widely. In 1957 he met with Vice-President Nixon, and in 1958 he conferred with President Eisenhower. He was becoming the pre-eminent black leader.

But King was simply the most visible champion of civil rights, a spokesman and symbol of the cause rather than its commander. In the late 1950s other leaders and organisations were flexing their muscles too, often in response to a black activism rooted in local communities, campuses and churches. The NAACP was pressing ahead with its court actions and with lobbying Congress for civil rights laws. Two civil rights acts were passed in 1957 and 1960, far weaker than demanded but the first such legislation since Reconstruction and an uneasy acknowledgement by the white power structure of the growing expectations of African Americans. The Congress of Racial Equality (CORE), first established during the Second World War, revived and resumed its own direct action campaigns. In 1959 it began a sit-in at a lunch counter in Miami and launched a movement to desegregate the Miami beaches. When the Greensboro students sparked off the sit-ins of 1960, CORE stepped in to help.

After the sit-ins came the Freedom Rides, organised by James Farmer and CORE. Southern bus stations had always been segregated, with separate waiting rooms, bathrooms and eating places for the two races, where these facilities were provided for blacks at all. The Supreme Court in 1960 had already declared against such segregation without practical effect, but the ruling provided an opportunity for CORE to act knowing that the law was on its side, and it decided to send a group of activists on a bus journey through the South to test the terminals. Farmer anticipated that the riders would be arrested, and he hoped to fill up the jails until the South was forced to abandon segregation, as he also hoped to pressure the Kennedy administration into decisive support for civil rights. The thirteen Freedom Riders, white and black, set off in two buses in May 1961, and others joined them along the way. Most were young graduates of the sit-ins, leavened by a few older people. The American Nazi Party retaliated by sending a 'hate bus' on its own journey through the South.

Cities in the Upper South obligingly desegregated their terminals to greet the Freedom Riders, but as they reached into the Deep South the atmosphere grew uglier. One bus was firebombed outside Anniston, Alabama. In Birmingham riders on the other bus were viciously attacked by whites; an FBI agent reported that he 'couldn't see their faces through the blood'. Although the estimated time of arrival of the bus was widely known, there were no police in evidence – they were later said to be visiting their mothers on Mothers' Day. CORE was reluctantly obliged to end the protest when no bus was prepared to take the riders further, but a few days later SNCC assembled some new riders, who boldly set out from Birmingham for Montgomery. The worried Kennedy administration sent two senior officials from the Justice Department to Alabama in the hope that their presence would discourage violence, but to no avail. When the riders arrived in Montgomery a mob again attacked as police stood by, and one of the Kennedy emissaries was himself beaten unconscious. (After an ambulance was slow to reach him, police explained that every white ambulance in town had broken down.) And still the riders pressed on into the yet Deeper South, though intense pressure from the Kennedys on Mississippi's political chieftains averted further serious violence, even if many riders had to spend time in the state's unfriendly jails. The Freedom Rides of May and June 1961 were a stunning public relations success for the campaigners. Photographic and television pictures of the burnings, beatings and arrests were relayed across the world. As James Farmer later explained, 'we were counting on the bigots in the South to do our work for us'.

Shamed by the ugliness of the violence and cowed by the threat of legal action, most southern bus, rail and air terminals soon submitted to an order of the Interstate Commerce Commission to end segregation. The wider objectives of securing public attention and energising the civil rights movement were also largely accomplished. The rides exposed the viciousness of southern white racism before the whole nation and seared the conscience of many citizens. The sit-ins and freedom rides also rather suddenly revealed the potential of peaceful direct action for challenging discrimination. It had been one thing to boycott a bus company and quite another bodily to confront the oppressor, with the attendant risks to life and freedom. Yet the participants had also grasped that the federal authorities could not allow widespread violence against blacks. This perception inspired further protests through the mid-1960s.

Protests of various kinds were now surfacing in many communities, even in the Deep South. When the black veteran, James Meredith, attempted to enrol in the University of Mississippi in 1962, backed by a federal court order, no less a figure than the governor of the state, Ross Barnett, stood at the door to stop him. Mob violence escalated, claiming two lives, forcing President Kennedy to despatch Army troops, itself an escalation of the role of federal authority in the civil rights cause. Meredith went about his studies at 'Ole Miss' under their protection. He was to make another courageous individual stand in 1966 when he embarked on a lone march across Mississippi to encourage local African Americans to claim the right to vote. After Meredith was injured in a shotgun attack the national civil rights leadership took over the march, although it was to reveal an emerging schism between moderates like Martin Luther King and the radicals of SNCC.

But that was in the future. After the spontaneity of the sit-ins and the panache of the Freedom Rides, the civil rights groups were searching for more deliberate strategies to destroy Jim Crow. Turning their attention to a whole community, SNCC and SCLC led a campaign in 1961–2 for the integration of public places in Albany, Georgia. The movement failed, partly because of divisions among the campaigners, but more because of the canny actions of the Albany police chief, who successfully prevailed on his officers to refrain from overt violence and to make arrests only on defensible charges. King and his friend Ralph Abernathy, in the latter's words, at one point were 'thrown out of jail' so that they would not become martyrs. Since order in the city was more-or-less maintained and the Constitution was not egregiously defied, a relieved federal government was not obliged to intervene and the Albany authorities could simply ignore the demands to integrate.

King then determined on a major campaign against segregation in Birmingham, Alabama, widely regarded as the most racist city in the South. Storming this citadel would surely spell the end to Jim Crow everywhere. This was to be 'Project C' (or Confrontation), for public order in the city was the responsibility of the hard-line police commissioner, Eugene 'Bull' Connor, and the protest marches and sit-ins were likely to encounter his hostility. The object was to force the Kennedy administration into a more vigorous commitment to civil rights. King was arrested in April 1963, and from his cell he issued his moving 'Letter from Birmingham Jail', in which he insisted that non-violent action was not causing tension but lancing it, exposing injustice 'to the light of human conscience and the air of national opinion'. When the supply of black adults willing to go to jail began to thin and media attention began to flag, their place was taken by children, hundreds and hundreds of whom offered themselves to Bull Connor's disconcerted police in the cause of freedom.

As Connor's exasperation grew, and as the mass action began to overwhelm the authorities, city police officers showed less restraint, and they finally used powerful fire hoses, clubs and Alsatian dogs on the demonstrators. Pictures of savage police dogs lunging at children were relayed around the world. The frenetic attempts by SCLC organisers to dissuade Birmingham's blacks from themselves resorting to violence sent another message to governmental officials – if the kind of leadership personified by Martin Luther King lost its hold in the black community, American streets could run with blood. The implacable demands of Birmingham's blacks, plunging sales in the downtown stores, the deteriorating public image of the city, and pressure from Robert Kennedy's Justice Department finally caused the local business community to buckle, and in May it reached a compromise with the SCLC. This did not end the tension in the city, as bomb blasts and other forms of violence testified to the precariousness of order. But an aroused public opinion in the country at large and continuing presidential pressure ensured a grudging desegregation of public facilities. The hate in the city was illustrated in September when four little black girls were killed in a bomb attack on their Sunday school.

Following the SCLC success in Birmingham in May, other protests rippled across the South. Perhaps a thousand demonstrations – sit-ins, marches, boycotts – illustrated the new activism of southern blacks that summer. Some remained peaceful, and several towns integrated their public facilities, but in others demonstrators were clubbed, tear-gassed or arrested. Medgar Evers, NAACP's leader in Mississippi, was murdered. Between April and November 1963 the Southern Regional Council counted 15,000 arrests arising from demonstrations, in which perhaps a 100,000 people participated. The civil rights cause was becoming a mass movement, and one moreover which engaged the sympathy of a great many white Americans as well as black. To many, in the summer of 1963 the country seemed to be teetering on the edge of race war. The Kennedy administration had little alternative but to give civil rights its most urgent attention.

During his first two years in the White House, as discussed in chapter 3, Kennedy had prudently sought to advance the cause of civil rights through executive action rather than legislation. But the growing protests and violence in the South forced his hand: he could no longer steer an uncertain middle way between his African American and his southern white constituents. Early in 1963 Kennedy had sent a mild civil rights bill to Congress, but after the bloodshed of the early summer, especially the disturbing events in Birmingham, he called for a stronger measure. In June, as Governor Wallace was standing at the door of the University of Alabama to block the admission of two black students, President Kennedy spoke to the nation on television to insist that blacks could no longer be appeased with 'counsels of patience' and that 'race has no place in American life or law'. The weight of the presidency was finally being put behind the civil rights movement, and a week later Kennedy sent to Congress a bill designed to eliminate segregation in the South in almost every public sphere.

To encourage Congress to pass the bill, the civil rights groups co-operated in organising the great March on Washington of August 1963, mobilising 200,000 blacks and perhaps 50,000 whites. Labour leaders, church leaders, film stars and musicians lent their support to the occasion, which was consummated by Martin Luther King's celebrated 'I Have A Dream' speech, in which he anticipated the day when 'all God's children, black men and white men, Jews and gentiles, Protestants and Catholics, will be able to join hands and sing in the words of the old Negro spiritual: "Free at last. Free at last. Thank God Almighty, we are free at last".' If black radicals were not altogether enchanted by the warm-hearted rhetoric, the march had helped solidify moderate Americans throughout the country behind the cause.

But it did not change many votes in Congress. The majority of senators and congressmen had been persuaded of the need for the civil rights bill, but the white South's unreconstructed representatives remained unrelenting in their hostility, and they could still mount a wrecking filibuster in the senate. Fate took a mordant hand. In November John Kennedy was assassinated in Dallas, a city in which hatred for his civil rights policies was intense. The popular wave which then developed in favour of sustaining the programme of the martyred president and the parliamentary skills of his successor together ensured that the civil rights bill became law in July 1964. Jim Crow had finally been outlawed in the American South.

The act struck primarily at segregation in public places, such as hotels, sports grounds, restaurants and cinemas, established an Equal Employment Opportunity Commission to curb discrimination in employment, increased the powers of the Attorney General to intervene in desegregation suits, and authorised the withholding of federal funds from public programmes in which discrimination persisted. To the surprise of many, the integration of public facilities proceeded fairly swiftly and with little trouble; local authorities often moved quickly to ensure that their entitlements to federal grants were not endangered. Of course, the prohibition of Jim Crow did not end discrimination in the South. For one thing, the act made only a modest attempt to guarantee voting rights.

In the early 1960s SNCC and other civil rights groups, with some support from the Kennedy administration, had organised a Voter Education Project, or voter registration drive. The deepest of Deep Southern states were Mississippi and Alabama, but as the drive took off there in 1962 it soon became clear that the activists risked their lives, and white brutality effectively put an end to the project. But SNCC was not easily intimidated, and it continued to search for ways of raising the consciousness of blacks in Mississippi. As national public sympathy for civil rights grew in 1963, and encouraged by the effectiveness of direct action in Birmingham, SNCC persuaded CORE, the SCLC and the NAACP to join it in the formation of a Council of Federated Organisations and a renewed attempt at voter registration. When northern white students joined the campaign it was noted that they attracted media attention. Such attention was needed, and when SNCC in 1964 announced a major registration drive, known as Freedom Summer, it encouraged white students to participate. As one organiser later starkly explained, the 'death of a white college student would bring on more attention to what was going on than for a black college student getting it'. Over a thousand students (more whites than blacks) from the North poured into Mississippi to assist, entreating dubious rural blacks to register and offering their children a fresh form of American history and civics in 'freedom schools'. They did something to break down the deferential attitudes of many black Mississippians. The failure of the Johnson administration to send federal marshals to protect the volunteers – it denied it had the constitutional authority to act pre-emptively – embittered some black leaders. There were many violent incidents, the most notorious being the horrific murders of three volunteers, two of them white. During the course of the summer COFO estimated that it had registered 1200 blacks in Mississippi at the cost of six deaths.

The Johnson administration could not ignore these well-publicised atrocities – for once the FBI made a determined effort to identify the killers of the three volunteers – but moderate civil rights groups and the White House had also been exasperated by the dangerous nature of the Mississippi project, and it took another campaign fully to establish the moral urgency of voting rights. This was the initiative of Martin Luther King Jr, who decided to focus his attention on a single town rather than a whole state. In the spring of 1965 he skilfully orchestrated a voter registration campaign in Selma, Alabama, deploying his philosophy of non-violent resistance to preserve peaceful behaviour among the protesters while courting violence by whites. King's colleague, Hosea Williams, told a group of marchers that 'We must pray, in God's name, for the white man to commit violence, and *we must not fight back!*' Some black militants felt that King did not push his confrontational tactics far enough, as when he turned back a march at one point rather than breach a federal court order, but he won the vital battle for public opinion. As in Birmingham, an obligingly belligerent police chief, Jim Clark, aided the strategy, among other instruments deploying electric cattle prods, and the media was able to project an image of African Americans as the innocent victims of white brutality. Public opinion and the federal government could only condemn white violence and endorse the civil rights cause. With the powerful support of Lyndon Johnson, a voting rights bill sped through Congress. This act was to prove effective, particularly because of its provision to send federal registrars if necessary into the South to do the registering. In Selma in 1966 newly-enfranchised black voters helped to turn Jim Clark out of office.

Apart from leading to a dramatic rise in the registration of black voters, the Voting Rights Act was an important symbolic confirmation that African Americans were fully citizens of the United States. In that sense it represented the consummation of the civil rights movement, a movement that focused on the constitutional rights of the individual. The acts of 1964 and 1965 enshrined the goals of the civil rights cause, publicly proclaiming an end to segregation and discrimination in the South. While reality limped behind legislation, by the mid-1960s liberal reformers (both in the civil rights movement and in the political community associated with the New Deal Order) could feel that their strategy was succeeding. In a remarkably few years they had destroyed the foundations of a caste system that had lasted for generations.

Yet the limitations of the strategy of integration were showing. Desegregation was patchy, the commitment of Washington was open to question, and the agenda of the civil rights movement had limited applicability to northern blacks. Further, the escalating war in Vietnam was distracting media and governmental attention and providing an alternative cause for white campus rebels. And at the moment of its success the civil rights movement was being sundered by the emergence of black nationalism. The various organisations – the NAACP, SCLC, CORE, the Urban League, SNCC – had never found it easy to work together. To the extent that they each possessed different priorities they could pursue complementary missions, and their leaders generally recognised that they needed one another and co-operated where they could. But their differing philosophies were also a source of tension, and civil rights issues allowed no ready demarcation. The frequent necessity for compromise – not only between the various groups but also to accommodate federal and local governmental officials – often left sour tempers and bruised egos. A number of SNCC members had come away from the March on Washington bitter at the way in which their spokesman John Lewis had been pressured into moderating his speech at the Lincoln Memorial. When Martin Luther King abided by an understanding with the Johnson White House to turn around a march at Selma rather than again confront state troopers, more militant blacks felt betrayed. While King tried to keep open channels of communication with the Johnson administration, by 1965 SNCC and CORE leaders were angering it by criticising its Vietnam policy. If the civil rights movement had succeeded in winning its major legislative goals with the historic acts of 1964 and 1965, the struggle had also helped to radicalise many black activists who were growing impatient with the pacifist and assimilationist philosophy of Martin Luther King. 'Integration is a subterfuge for the maintenance of white supremacy', argued Stokely Carmichael in 1966.

There always had been some black radicals who had held aloof from the mainstream civil rights movement. In the 1930s the Nation of Islam took uncertain root in northern black ghettos, promoting notions that blacks were God's chosen people and that Christianity was a white man's creed foisted on blacks to control them. The Black Muslims, as they were known, were led by Elijah Muhammad, who spoke of whites as 'blue-eyed devils' and who enjoyed particular success among the rootless urban underclass. By the late 1950s Nation of Islam membership was escalating towards 50,000. By Christian standards, the Muslims embraced a distinctly puritanical life-style, abjuring drugs, alcohol and tobacco, working hard, dressing soberly, and developing their own businesses. Many former criminals, drug addicts and prostitutes found in this discipline a positive structure for their lives.

One of those to be captivated by the Black Muslim faith while in prison was Malcolm Little, who was reborn as Malcolm X and who rapidly became one of the Nation's most charismatic leaders. Highly intelligent and quick-witted, Malcolm scorned what he saw as the accommodationist strategy of the civil rights movement, insisted that the white man was the enemy, and called for the 'absolute separation of the black and white races' with a rhetoric that hinted at revolution. By 1964 he had come to overshadow Elijah Muhammed and a breach occurred between them, resulting in Malcolm leaving the Nation of Islam and seeking a way to articulate his own nationalist philosophy. In April he talked of blacks forming 'rifle clubs' for self-defence, and that summer he formed the Organisation for Afro-American Unity. A visit to Mecca seemed to encourage him to espouse the equality of all races, including whites. By this date, still lacking a coherent strategy and estranged from the Muslims, Malcolm's support among African Americans was limited, but early in 1965 he was assassinated, and in his martyrdom he bequeathed to American blacks not a programme but an image of militancy and a powerful vision of black pride. As one SNCC leader commented, in Malcolm blacks saw 'a living link between Africa and the civil rights movement in this country'.

Malcolm X was a voice from the black ghetto rather than the black South. The growth of the Black Muslims in the northern cities, with their hostility towards whites and their separatist philosophy, had already suggested that not all urban blacks would place much confidence in mere changes in the law. The cities were already beginning to rumble. In July 1964, following speculation of a 'long, hot summer', Harlem had exploded, in the same month blacks in Rochester took to the streets, and there were eruptions that summer too in Jersey City, Paterson, Chicago, and Philadelphia. These were to prove but the first of the 'summer riots' of the 1960s. The horrendous week-long Watts riot followed in 1965, Chicago and Cleveland in 1966, and Newark and Detroit a year later. In 1968, on 4 April, Martin Luther King Jr was assassinated, and within minutes of the news being broadcast African Americans were taking to the streets. Riots broke out in over a hundred cities, and within a week forty-six people died and 27,000 were arrested. Over 700 fires lit up Washington D. C.

The liberalism associated with the New Deal Order and the civil rights movement had not provided an answer for this black anger. As southern blacks had fled to the northern ghettos, they had become the victims of a range of economic and social pressures supplementing those of race. The civil rights legislation had served to raise black expectations, but in the urban North conditions were often deteriorating, and the acts of the mid-1960s offered no remedies. The systemic racism of northern cities was more difficult to confront than the legal racism of the South. For the most part the ghetto riots were not planned, but they were a measure of the bitterness that existed. And as urban blacks became more insistent in their demands for improvement, suburban whites grew more worried. Many middle-class whites had campaigned for integration in the South; they seemed less receptive to demands for open housing and an end to *de facto* school segregation in the North. African American claims encountered an increasingly hostile white backlash, which could only serve to erode race relations yet further. Some blacks were concluding that what was needed was not new legislation but a fundamental restructuring of the economic system, and to a few it seemed that there was no political alternative to violence.

For some black leaders events at the 1964 Democratic national convention had been a turning point. SNCC activists in Mississippi had been instrumental in forming the Mississippi Freedom Democratic Party (MFDP), a black counterpart to the regular (white) Democratic party, and it sent delegates to the national convention. It had expected at least some support from the Johnson White House which had just pushed the civil rights act through Congress, but Johnson, anxious to avoid a major floor fight with white southerners, decided to back the party regulars. White liberals like Hubert Humphrey and Walter Reuther tried to devise a compromise, but while their plan offered a better deal for black delegates in the future it allowed for only token representation at the 1964 convention and the MFDP angrily rejected it. Earlier that month widespread publicity had been accorded to the discovery of the mutilated bodies of three Freedom Summer volunteers; it seemed that their sacrifice had been in vain. To SNCC leaders the spurning of the MFDP was evidence of the inherent racism of the political establishment and the untrustworthiness of white liberals.

From out of the frustration with conventional political action came the concept of Black Power. The phrase came into use in 1966, when it was popularised by people like the Harlem Congressman Adam Clayton Powell and SNCC leader Stokely Carmichael. The 'black power' demand was much more provocative than the old demand for 'freedom'. Designed as a battle cry to mark a break with the old civil rights movement, it seemed to mean separatism, a repudiation of any co-operation with white society, and integrationist leaders like Roy Wilkins of the NAACP and Martin Luther King disliked it. Instead of assimilation into the mainstream, the slogan suggested, blacks should build a separate, autonomous community, unified along racial lines, in order to force concessions from whites. The recent securing of independence by several African countries suggested the potential of black solidarity.

One of the virtues of the term Black Power was its ambiguity, and even moderate blacks could explore the implication that there was a distinctive black identity. The concept encouraged interest in African traditions and the African American heritage and served powerfully to promote black pride. 'Black is beautiful' was the cry as blacks emphasised their racial characteristics, spurning the hair straighteners and skin bleaches of the previous generation and instead growing Afro haircuts and celebrating black music and soul food. One of the most electrifying of consciousness-raising actions, seen on television and film by young people of all races around the world, was the Black Power salute given by two African American medallists at the Mexico City Olympics in

1968. Black Power helped to bring about a kind of psychological revolution among many blacks. Long taught to believe themselves to be inferior, they now took joy in their blackness. Further, Black Power directed responsibility for deprivation towards whites. If black was beautiful, it followed that the conditions under which blacks lived were not their fault.

From the mid-1960s the more radical black groups began to deploy the slogan of Black Power, although they were unfortunate in their timing, for the ghetto riots imparted violent overtones to the concept. SNCC leaders edged away from reform alliances after the 1964 Democratic Convention, with its failure to seat the black Mississippi delegates. The election of Stokely Carmichael as chairman in May 1966 signalled SNCC's repudiation of integrationism: 'We reject the American dream as defined by white people, and must work to construct an American reality defined by Afro-Americans'. In December its executive committee expelled its white members. By 1967 H. Rap Brown was SNCC's chief spokesman, and as violence against blacks increased in that hate-filled summer he advised: 'Meet violence with violence'. CORE followed a somewhat similar trajectory. The black nationalist Floyd McKissick replaced the integrationist James Farmer as national director in 1966, and in 1967 he spoke of revolution as a constitutional right. White participation in CORE activities was falling markedly in the mid-1960s, and in 1967 it removed the term 'multiracial' in its definition of its membership. But white liberals (not least New York Jews) had helped these groups financially, and funding dwindled markedly as their exclusivity and militancy grew. Moderate groups were as wary of the black nationalists as the militants were of them. In July 1966 the NAACP decided to end any links with SNCC and CORE.

Another variant of black radicalism was the Black Panther Party for Self-Defense, founded in September 1966 in Oakland, California, calling for a revolutionary reconstruction of American society. The Panthers' black berets and jackets and their introduction of armed patrols in the ghettos (to keep an eye on the white police) captured press attention. In 1968 a short-lived alliance was formed between the Black Panthers and SNCC, Stokely Carmichael becoming the Panther prime minister. By 1969 the Panthers were claiming chapters in several large cities, and if small in individual numbers they had won a lot of publicity and some followers in the ghettos.

But they were also rent by division, and they could be confused with other elements more explicitly advocating violence, such as the Black Liberation Front. The Panthers' philosophy was Marxist, but much modified by the realities of the American environment; Eldridge Cleaver described it as 'a Yankee-Doodle-Dandy version of socialism'. In order to build community support, the Panthers engaged in local programmes, such as providing free breakfasts for poor children and legal assistance for blacks entangled with the police. They also – as socialists – accepted the need to forge class alliances with other groups, including whites and Puerto Ricans. One issue on which they on occasion made common cause was resistance to the Vietnam War. But if the Panthers were trying to shake off their reputation for violence, it came too late. The authorities had taken them at their own estimation as the vanguard of revolution, and, as previously noted, during the early years of the Nixon administration the Panthers were decimated by arrests and shootings.

The FBI may have seen the Black Panthers as the greatest threat to American security, but there were black militants more committed to violence. The Revolutionary Action Movement and the Black Liberation Army, for example, doubted whether the Panthers would be able to survive police repression and developed theories in which revolution would be achieved via underground warfare, much as Third World nationalists were seeking to throw off their imperialist oppressors. These urban warriors would train in secret and strike at night at the institutions of white society, disabling communication systems, blowing up major industrial plants, firing cities, and leading the black masses in an uprising against the government. Such scenarios never went much beyond rhetoric, but there was enough to trigger raids against those held to be engaged in such plots. J. Edgar Hoover told a congressional sub-committee in 1967 that the Revolutionary Action Movement was a 'highly secret all-Negro, Marxist-Leninist, Chinese Communist-oriented' group 'dedicated to the overthrow of the capitalist system in the United States, by violence if necessary'.

The various black militant groups commanded abundant press coverage but made little political headway and lacked access to legitimate funds. One problem was continued conflict between themselves, especially between those totally opposed to working with whites and those prepared to ally with radical white groups. Crucially, the militants failed to win over the mass of African Americans. In embracing revolution they marginalized themselves. Their organisations were also subject to extensive police harassment and to subversion by FBI moles, and by the early 1970s they were collapsing. SNCC had gone out of existence, CORE was a minority sect, and the Black Panthers had all but disappeared. In an opinion poll of the summer of 1970 some 75 per cent of respondents reported a 'Highly Unfavorable' view of the Black Panthers – the same proportion as for the Ku Klux Klan.

The militant turn weakened the mainstream civil rights movement but did not destroy it. Conscious of the racial tensions in the northern cities and worried about the implications of black nationalism, Martin Luther King determined to apply his non-violent philosophy to Chicago, hoping to find ways of unpicking the city's extensive de facto segregation. In January 1966 he launched a campaign to improve ghetto housing, persuading a number of tenants to withhold rents. In August King led a march into a white ethnic neighbourhood, where the marchers encountered unnerving hostility as onlookers screamed abuse and threw stones. But Mayor Daley was somewhat unnerved too as the SCLC threatened to continue its marches in unfriendly territory, and fearing for the reputation of his city he offered a plan to end residential segregation. This was a far-reaching promise that King accepted, although the means of its accomplishment remained unclear and it was at best a symbolic victory. Somewhat more heartening was the progress of Operation Breadbasket, led by King's young associate Jesse Jackson, a consumer boycott of local retailers to persuade them to employ more blacks. In about a year some 2,000 jobs were secured for blacks, a worthy achievement though hardly enough to dent ghetto poverty.

The SCLC's attempts to address the problems of Chicago were disappointing. Its limited resources were no match for the sheer size of the city, and in marked contrast to its southern campaigns there was little hope of bringing the pressure of the federal government to bear against the city's powerful Democratic machine. The city police had behaved with restraint, and King had been unable to mobilise public opinion and federal authority against Chicago's more-or-less legal segregation.

Meanwhile the continued escalation of the war in Vietnam and the failure of Lyndon Johnson's Great Society to deliver substantial benefits to poor blacks served to deepen the divisions both between the protest groups and between the old civil rights leadership and the White

House. 'In a real sense', observed Martin Luther King in April 1967, 'the Great Society has been shot down on the battlefields of Vietnam'. Yet Vietnam was a problem for civil rights activists. While the war extravagantly expended resources, including the lives of blacks who were more likely to be drafted – and killed in action – than whites, speaking out against government policy risked the wrath of an administration that had given unusual support to civil rights objectives. The more militant groups, pursuing their various nationalist trajectories, naturally turned against the war, the SNCC in particular early adopting a high profile anti-war stance. But the NAACP and the Urban League agonisingly strove to sustain a relationship with the president. Vietnam was sundering the civil rights movement as well as depriving it of potential support as white students in particular turned their energies to the anti-war cause. Martin Luther King for his part became increasingly critical of American policy, earning the censure of both black and white moderates.

By the late 1960s, even as he reaffirmed his commitment to integration, King's analysis of the problems confronting African Americans was not so different from some versions of Black Power ideology. Jesse Jackson's Operation Breadbasket might find jobs for a few thousand blacks, but how were the millions to be given a decent life? How were the ghettos to be quieted without federal governmental intervention? King was questioning the nature of the capitalist economy, and if he had no easy answers he was contemplating massive government programmes to provide jobs, a guaranteed decent minimum wage, and other means of extensively redistributing wealth. Most Americans would call this socialism.

But the capitalist system was not going to reconstruct itself. King finally determined to move from protest to prolonged civil disobedience, developing a plan to bring thousands of poor people of all races to Washington, where they would camp until the government acted. Not all of King's associates were enthusiastic about the Poor People's Campaign, with its ambitious logistical demands and its risk of provoking a backlash, and its launch date in Washington was deferred. In April 1968 King flew to Memphis to support a strike of black sanitation workers, hoping that the occasion might also mark the start of the Poor People's Campaign. 'I may not get there with you', he told a black audience, 'but I want you to know tonight that we as a people will get to the promised land'. He was assassinated by a white man the next day.

In the dispirited aftermath of the murder the SCLC did attempt to go ahead with the Poor People's Campaign, but the management was muddled, order proved difficult to maintain, and turnout was disappointing. Fires had burned across Washington on news of King's death, and the authorities were unmoved by further protests in the city. But King's martyrdom had brought one morsel to the civil rights cause. In January the administration had introduced a civil rights bill, an open housing measure, but its prospects in a Congress subject to the white backlash had not seemed good. Following the murder the bill unexpectedly sped into law, one designed to end discrimination in the sale or rental of housing. But the act also reflected the instincts of a suspicious Congress in introducing severe penalties for those implicated in riots.

Even before his death King had lost some of his authority as a civil rights leader, and no-one replaced him as the pre-eminent spokesman for the cause. The loose coalition of civil rights organisations which had attacked the white South had already fallen apart. It was difficult for the surviving integrationist groups to maintain momentum in the absence of a clearly-defined target and in the face of growing white antipathy, and the election of Richard Nixon meant that they could expect little succour from the White House. The Kennedys may have worried about the black vote, but Nixon understood that he had more to gain from the white backlash. Sapping the African American cause too was a growing pessimism among blacks. In 1964 a poll showed that 45 per cent reckoned that they 'usually get to carry out things their way'; by 1970 the figure had dropped to 23 per cent. Protest of itself, it seemed, was no longer enough, as King himself had recognised in his last months, arguing: 'We will have to build far-flung, workmanlike and experienced organisations ... if the legislation we create and the agreements we forge are to be ably and zealously superintended'. But painstaking organisation and institutionalisation would take time. Some blacks did throw their energies into other bodies that emerged from the Sixties ferment, such as the National Welfare Rights Organization. For many black militants King's assassination was proof enough that African Americans could not work with white America, but their own radical strategies lacked wide appeal.

Some took hope in the cultural strivings encouraged by the concept of Black Power. Among the more militant of the black cultural nationalist groups was US Organisation, based in Los Angeles and led by Maulana Ron Karenga. US believed that a cultural revolution had to precede a political revolution, that African Americans had to cast off white values and cultural forms and embrace an Afro-centric culture, such as by adopting Afro clothing and hairstyles and where possible the Swahili language. Karenga championed the celebration of *Kwanzaa* as an alternative to the white Christmas, first celebrated in Los Angeles at the end of December 1966, and soon popular in black households through the country. As black enrolment at colleges expanded, demands for 'black studies' were increasingly made and were often met. Black history came to be taught in schools and colleges, providing the rising generation with a strengthened sense of the African American heritage. Black culture in a variety of forms was achieving a momentum of its own. Not all black nationalists welcomed this emphasis on the primacy of culture and consciousness. Some saw the cultural route, as some white radicals saw the hippie counter-culture, as undermining the revolution.

Other African American activists were turning to conventional politics. Scores of moderates saw the militant stance of the black nationalists as liable to provoke repression, and worked instead to make use of the voting rights that had now been guaranteed, building their own organisations and fielding their own candidates where they could. White leaders became less acceptable to black communities. The Voting Rights Act did bring more blacks to the polls in the South, while the increasing concentration of blacks in the inner cities in the North enhanced their electoral power in local politics. Slowly the number of elected black politicians increased, bringing with them their own 3priorities. Black mayors appeared in northern cities, beginning with Cleveland and Gary in 1967. Where blacks won local office there were often material gains, such as improved street paving and lighting and better garbage collection. In 1965 there were fewer than 500 elected black officials in the entire United States; by 1989 there were over 7,000. African Americans even made political headway in the South. In 1964 only 40 per cent of eligible southern blacks were registered to vote; by 1970 the per centage had jumped to 65, and the proportion continued to rise thereafter. They increasingly elected some of their own to office, and by the 1970s southern blacks were beginning to appear in Congress. Even George Wallace began to apologise for his earlier stands and he respectfully wooed black voters when he sought election as governor of Alabama yet again in 1982.

The civil rights movement of the Sixties had destroyed the fortifications of the white South and had placed the power of the law behind black rights. The American creed of legal equality of opportunity had been extended to African Americans, however imperfectly, and greater numbers were soon moving up educational, occupational and political ladders. Even Lyndon Johnson's ill-fated Community Action Programs had done something to train a new generation of black leaders in the northern cities, and in Congress the Black Caucus came to exercise an influence that could not be ignored. The Black Power movement had generated a powerful sense of black identity and imparted a new energy to a vibrant black culture, which itself was to exercise a lasting challenge to the values of mainstream America. The dynamics of the American economy, however, continued to frustrate the aspirations of the majority of African Americans, and a growing gulf opened up between upwardly mobile blacks and the deprived masses. In this sense, the socioeconomic profile of African Americans was moving a little closer to that of white Americans, who had long been divided between a highly privileged few and a modestly-resourced many.

But the civil rights and Black Power movements had also served to sharpen a general awareness of rights and entitlements. White America had been forced to surrender some of its authority, and ethnic, gender and cultural groups of many kinds were being emboldened to assert their identities. The black revolt had spearheaded the attack on the traditional power structure, but arguably other groups were to benefit more from its dismantling.

CHAPTER 7

Protest: Youth, Peace and Women's Movements

Much of the academic and popular literature of the 1950s conveyed the impression that the 'typical' American was white, suburban, and middle-class, and indeed male. Images of the 'man in the gray flannel suit' competed with images of 'the organisation man' and images of the 'white-collar American' as characterisations of American identity. On television Robert Young portrayed a benign insurance manager in *Father Knows Best*, presiding over a wholesome middle-class family, and James Arness embodied manly values as Matt Dillon keeping the peace in *Gunsmoke*. In film a harassed Jim Backus, an apron over his businessman's suit, struggled to communicate with his erring son in *Rebel Without a Cause*, and a patient Henry Fonda coaxed justice from an all white and all male jury in *Twelve Angry Men*.

Of course, it was not as simple as this. After all, the most popular television show of the 1950s, *I Love Lucy*, featured a Cuban (if still middle-class) bandleader, and James Dean's confused rebel projected an anguished impatience with suburban conformity. Nonetheless the images of a bland culture and a homogeneous social order were paralleled in political life by a high degree of bipartisanship and an agreement on the broad contours of domestic and foreign policies. Even when Lyndon Johnson was flung into the presidency he made the promotion and preservation of a political consensus his primary goal. Many historians in the early 1960s were still interpreting American history in consensual terms, emphasising the shared values of most Americans in the past, an absence of ideological polarities, and historical continuities.

Insofar as there was a homogeneous social order and a political consensus at the outset of the 1960s, these features could not be readily discerned in the United States over which Richard Nixon presided.

American society, it was said, had 'come apart', and differentiation rather than uniformity continued to be seen as a dominant feature of American life. If American culture had once privileged the values of the white, professional middle class, in time politically-correct Americans would strive to celebrate their 'multicultural' society. Before he died John Kennedy had begun to emphasise the world's 'diversity'; he might have been speaking about the United States. The most devastating assault on the cosy world of white middle-class America had been mounted by African Americans, but they were not alone in pulling apart the old order.

The civil rights movement had successfully invaded the exposed conscience of white liberals, but it had also served to move others to action. A major inspiration behind Students for a Democratic Society (SDS), composed mainly of the heirs of the white middle class, was the sight of black students literally risking their lives in protest activity in the South. The non-violent protest philosophy of Martin Luther King made a powerful impression on many white Americans, although the more militant stance of black radicals could have a humbling effect on white activists too. When several radical groups held the National Conference for New Politics in Chicago in 1967, the white majority allowed the black minority to dictate the agenda. And black protest helped to inspire a range of liberation movements. The champions of other causes were emboldened by the courageous confrontation of southern racism by African Americans, they learned from the black movement how to mobilise and how to use the media, and they grasped too the need to frame their demands in terms of rights. The movement for women's liberation and the rights campaigns of Native Americans, Puerto Ricans, and others all owed something to the civil rights experience.

In no small part the protest and liberation movements of the Sixties were movements of the young. The four black students who sat at the Woolworth lunch-counter represented more than their race. 'Here were four students from Greensboro who were suddenly all over *Life* magazine', recalled a white founder of the SDS: 'There was a feeling that they were us and we were them, and a recognition that they were expressing something we were feeling as well'. Some young people sought an outlet for their energies in the Peace Corps, but for others the idealism of the New Frontier triggered an impatience with the status quo. The New Left, the anti-war movement, women's liberation, consumer and environmental protest and other movements too drew much of their energy from the younger generation. (So did the armed forces – the average age of soldiers in Vietnam was 19 and some were even younger, while in the Second World War the average age had been 26.)

The protest movements had their elders too, although these were rarely grey-haired. Michael Harrington, whose book *The Other America* helped to inspire the War on Poverty, was all of 34 when he attended the SDS's Port Huron convention. Ralph Nader, who gathered around himself a group of student volunteers known as Nader's Raiders to investigate unsafe products, was 31 when he first directed public attention to defective automobiles. Betty Friedan probably did not think of herself as old when she published *The Feminine Mystique* in her early 40s. Among the inspirational figures of young America, Malcolm X was 39 when he was gunned down, as was Martin Luther King, and Robert Kennedy was 42. Of course, the role of youth should not be exaggerated. Grandparents joined marches too, callused veterans of the labour movement often lent their support, and civil rights groups drew on the experience of seasoned foes of segregation. An important anti-war group was Women Strike for Peace, which consisted largely of middle-aged mothers. But the protest movements of the Sixties could not have achieved the momentum they did without the mobilisation of thousands of young people.

There were more of them: about a third of the Americans living in 1961 had been born since 1945. In the twenty years before 1960 the number of young people in the 15 to 24 age group had remained fairly stable, at around 23 or 24 million; by 1970 the figure had soared to over 35 million. In 1955 there had been 8.5 million Americans aged between 18 and 21; in 1965 there were 12.1 million and the number was growing. An astonishing and increasing proportion was reaching higher education. The number of students swelled from 2.3 million in 1950 to 3.6 million in 1960. The post-war baby boom was hitting the campuses by the mid-1960s; by 1968 there were over 6 million enrolled students and 8.6 million in 1970. By this date over 35 per cent of the relevant age group was attending college, compared to 22 per cent at the beginning of the decade.

As this tidal wave of young Americans hit the colleges they turned them into different kinds of places. While small colleges survived, many campuses were no longer the small communities of the past. There were only ten in 1948 with more than 20,000 students; by 1967 there were fifty-five. As university and class sizes grew, personal contact between professor and student was eroded, and campuses were increasingly managed by bureaucratic structures, even as their residential arrangements created vital communities of the young. Students were often learning more from their peers than from their professors, although most were immune to radicalism. One estimate put the proportion of active radicals during the Sixties at 5 per cent, but in a campus of 20,000 that meant 1,000 students, quite enough to occupy an administration building.

By the time that the youthful John Kennedy was campaigning for the presidency, with his promise 'to get the country moving again', there were signs of restiveness on the campuses. In May 1960 thousands of students staged demonstrations at hearings of the House Un-American Activities Committee in San Francisco, HUAC having swooped on the Bay Area because of the support it had offered to the civil rights cause. At about the same time students, Quakers and others held vigils outside San Quentin prison against the scheduled execution of Caryl Chessman, who had been convicted on a kidnapping charge eleven years earlier but whose eloquent writings had made him an international *cause célèbre*. Some students were attracted to a re-emerging peace movement. In 1959 the Student Peace Union was formed, and by 1962, with seventy chapters and 3,500 members, it was larger than the more flamboyant Students for a Democratic Society. Not all of this activity was on the left. Students from forty-four colleges met in September 1960 to form Young Americans for Freedom, a conservative group that was to support Barry Goldwater for president in 1964.

The year 1960 also saw the birth of Students for a Democratic Society (SDS). Formerly the Student League for Industrial Democracy, itself a group of idealists within the venerable League for Industrial Democracy, the SDS quickly earned a reputation for dynamic student politics, although its recruits were mainly white and middle-class. 'We are people of this generation, bred in at least modern comfort, housed now in universities, looking uncomfortably to the world we inherit', it explained in 1962. This was one key to the youthful activism of the Sixties – the sense of guilt and the limited outlet for self-expression afforded by a bland affluent society.

The evolution of the SDS is inseparable from that of the New Left, the more amorphous movement that it helped to define. In June 1962

SDS representatives met at Port Huron, Michigan, together with delegates from other leftist groups such as SNCC, CORE, and the Student Peace Union. There they set out their views in the Port Huron Statement, largely drafted by Tom Hayden. This, in characteristic 1960s fashion, declared that SDS's mission was to create 'meaning in life that is personally authentic'. It set itself against the 'depersonalization' and bureaucratic traits of modern society, insisted on the potential within each individual for 'self-cultivation, self-direction, ... and creativity', and called for the revitalisation of American politics through 'participatory democracy'. The statement inveighed against racial bigotry, the constraints of the Cold War and the dependence on nuclear weapons, and poverty and unemployment. It saw reason for hope in the universities, which with their youthful clientele, internal dynamics and access to knowledge could become centres for radical change. The SDS looked to the emergence of a 'new left ... consisting of younger people', which would promote controversy in order to awaken Americans from a 'national apathy'.

Initially touched by New Frontier idealism, the emerging New Left was egalitarian and communitarian and suspicious of hierarchy and established institutions. Some participants took inspiration from the Beat sub-culture, with its defiance of authority and convention. The term New Left distanced the fledgling cause from the Marxist Old Left, with its preoccupation with economic class oppression, although several young activists sprang from liberal and radical homes. The Port Huron Statement directed attention instead to the 'mechanisms of psychological and cultural domination' deployed by late capitalist society. In 1963 the SDS moved further left when it distanced itself from the liberal Democrats: '... the capture of liberal rhetoric and the liberal power base by the corporate liberalism of the New Frontiersmen means that the reformers and the democratically oriented liberals are trapped by the limitations of the Democratic Party.' It was beginning consciously to turn against the Cold War consensus. The New Left looked to the liberation of the individual rather than of a class, a liberation that was at least in part psychological, a perspective that served to encourage the women's and gay liberation movements as they emerged.

But the SDS was influenced too by the quickening civil rights movement, as well as by its own roots in industrial democracy. Keen to work in the community, and inspired by SNCC's brave attempts at voter registration in the rural Deep South, SDS activists founded the

Economic Research and Action Project (ERAP). The urban poor – like southern blacks – they believed, had to be empowered. ERAP sent students into deprived districts in northern cities with a view to organising protest around local grievances and fashioning interracial coalitions of the poor. Between 1963 and 1965 about fifteen such projects were launched, with over a hundred students going to live in the slums of such cities as Boston, Cleveland and Chicago, involving themselves in such activities as helping welfare mothers and tenant associations to organise to press their demands. Women often assumed vital organisational roles in these projects, if this was not always recognised by the male SDS leaders on the campuses. But ERAP had been founded on the assumption that US capitalism was about to experience a sharp economic downturn, and that SDS would then be well placed to mobilise the unemployed. Yet in the mid-1960s the economy perversely boomed, Lyndon Johnson's War on Poverty began its own invasion of the slums, and by 1965 the ERAP projects were in decline.

By this date SDS was finding a new and powerful cause. Anti-war sentiment was growing. Lyndon Johnson had won the Gulf of Tonkin resolution from Congress in August 1964 and in February 1965 he launched the bombing campaign of North Vietnam; by April he had authorised US Marines to undertake offensive operations. There were a few liberal voices raised against this escalation, but too few to satisfy the restive idealists of SDS. 'We were outraged; isolated; suspicious of those who damned us or counselled caution', SDS leader Todd Gitlin remembered: 'The defaults and assaults of liberals and social democrats blew us leftward; so did SDS's increasingly plausible commitment to go it alone; so did the growing social base for alienation on the American campus'. 'Teach-ins' against the war spread across the nation's campuses following the example set at the University of Michigan in March, when 2,500 students attended lectures and rallies devoted to Vietnam. This was the first significant protest ever by American students against foreign policy. In April 1965 the SDS organised the first major protest against the war, the largest anti-war demonstration thus far in US history, a march on the White House attracting some 20,000 or more people, most of them students. This rally gave SDS national media attention. SDS membership grew fourfold between December 1964 and October 1965, when it reached 10,000. When SDS debated whether to launch an anti-draft campaign in the fall, branch membership swelled.

But with the anti-war expansion of 1965 the SDS's effectiveness peaked. A group committed to the principle of participatory democracy had always had its organisational difficulties, which were enhanced as the number of local chapters grew. At the same time this growth was bringing in new kinds of recruits, the so-called 'prairie power' members from the Midwest and Southwest, who were hostile to central leadership and keen to delegate control to local chapters, and the 'old guard' began to yield its positions. In that year the SDS also changed its constitution so that apologists for 'totalitarian' principles were no longer debarred, a stance that encouraged an infusion of members from the Marxist-Leninist Progressive Labor party. This reinforced the tendency towards schism and fragmentation. By 1966 the loose-knit SDS boasted some 151 chapters scattered across the nation's campuses. The number of individual SDS also members continued to grow, with up to 100,000 being claimed by the late Sixties. It is not clear how much they agreed on beyond the stance expressed in the slogan: 'Screw the ass of the ruling class'.

Though the most celebrated, the SDS was not the only student protest group. Indeed, students at the University of California at Berkeley had captured national press attention even before the SDS. A major demonstration erupted on the campus in September 1964, when the authorities prohibited the use of the Berkeley Strip (an area inside the main campus entrance) for recruitment for off-campus political activities. The Free Speech Movement dragged on and in December thousands of students occupied the administration building; their ejection by the police and 800 arrests brought yet further publicity. 'You can't trust anyone over thirty,' was one slogan thrown up by the FSM, itself largely led by young veterans of the civil rights movement. Shortly before the flare-up university president Clark Kerr had spoken of the 'knowledge industry' to which the vast University of California was dedicated, and its mission was to serve the national purpose. Intellect, he approvingly wrote, had even become 'a component part of the "military-industrial complex".' Student leader Mario Savio had a different view when he characterised the university as a machine and called on students to put their 'bodies against the gears, against the wheels and machines, and make it stop until we are free'. The students in fact won much faculty support and eventually the university conceded that there should be no restrictions on speech. But Berkeley students remained in the forefront of protest. There was another flare-up in March 1965 after a student was arrested for displaying a notice bearing the word 'fuck', and Berkeley then emerged as a centre of anti-war activity, which included obstructing troop trains by sitting on the tracks.

The Berkeley example helped to inspire other student demonstrations. There were frequent complaints about the impersonal and bureaucratic nature of large universities and about the paternalistic rules that often survived. At this time 21 was still the age of majority, so that universities served *in loco parentis* and regulated student conduct accordingly. Students normally had no formal role in university government, but notions of 'participatory democracy' encouraged them to demand a voice. More seriously, just as Clark Kerr was making connections between the university and the 'military-industrial complex', so were students. As unease over the Vietnam War grew, students became increasingly suspicious of the research contracts awarded to universities by government, some of which were for classified research for defence agencies. For radical students, universities were coming to stand for the enemy.

The various student and black radical groups associated with the New Left meant that it encompassed a range of disparate viewpoints, but the growing breach with liberal organisations pointed up its general stance. The New Left was positioning itself against the governing elites and major policies of American society. Where southern racists had once seemed to be the principal enemy of equality and decency, by the mid-1960s the target was the northern liberal or 'corporate liberalism'. What might be called 'the liberal establishment' was held to be adept at co-opting its potential critics, at quietly disarming those that might become arrayed against it. As Jack Newfield, an early member of the SDS, wrote in 1966, a principal obstacle to the New Left was 'the culture's spongelike genius for either absorbing or merchandising all dissent'. The elderly guru of the New Left, the philosopher Herbert Marcuse, spoke of modern society's capacity for 'repressive tolerance'.

Power in the United States resided ultimately in corporate capitalism, in the radical analysis, and through a host of formal and informal means the major corporations had harnessed the political institutions to their cause. These were not the ruthless, repressive capitalists of Old Left memory, but sophisticated operators who espoused liberal policies to win a measure of consensus for their agenda. They were happy enough to recognise trade unions and pay generous wages, thus recruiting labour to the consumer society, as they were also prepared to encourage government to provide a modicum of welfare services, which would maintain consumer spending and avert serious social divisions. But, according to New Left theorists, corporate liberalism could only go so far in offering benefits to the lower class, since profits had to be maintained and a surplus of labour had its uses. Lyndon Johnson's celebrated War on Poverty represented little more than a series of gestures to camouflage the essential inequalities of capitalist society. The Vietnam War too served the interests of corporate liberalism, for the corporations supplied the armaments, as in more general terms an imperialist policy would provide markets abroad. By 1965 many New Leftists were speaking of 'the system' on the one hand and 'the movement' on the other. Liberals were the agents of 'the system', whether wittingly or not, and in many ways more dangerous than unreconstructed reactionaries whose enmity was easily perceived. One radical leader in 1965 characterised the idea of working with liberal reformers as a 'coalition with the marines'.

By the mid-1960s too the 'counter-culture' was emerging to add to the appeal of the New Left for young people. The two were not synonymous, and many members of the New Left looked askance at the pot-smoking, bead necklaces and mysticism associated with the counter-culture. (The national SDS office was worried about the publicity following a drugs raid on a party in Norman, Oklahoma, in 1966, when some SDS members were among those arrested; two of the people charged were placed in a mental hospital for observation because of their long hair!) But if the New Left was defining itself in terms of opposition to 'the system', it seemed natural enough also to dissociate itself from the dominant culture. A folk singer entertained the marchers at the anti-war demonstration in Washington in April 1965 with a version of Bob Dylan's 'The Times They Are a-Changing'. At an anti-war demonstration at Berkeley in 1966 the protesters replaced the song 'Solidarity Forever' with the Beatles' 'Yellow Submarine', which supposedly celebrated psychedelic experiences. One root of the counter-culture was the Beat Generation, with their celebration of spontaneity, drugs and free love, and the bohemian communities found in Greenwich Village and San Francisco's Haight-Ashbury. Another was folk music, which had been reviving since the late 1950s and which, in its lyrics, lent itself to making a statement. By the mid-Sixties the Beatles and the Rolling Stones were introducing rebellious notes into pop music. It was in 1965 that Bob Dylan, who had attended an SDS meeting, switched from folk songs to his distinctive brand of folkrock music, with its more political content, reaching No. 1 with 'Like a Rolling Stone'. In the early days of the New Left there had been attempts to make connections with labour groups such as the United Auto Workers, and the labour movement had long been associated with a folk music tradition. The displacement of folk music by rock music in the mid-1960s paralleled the New Left's abandonment of co-operation with older reform and labour groups.

The counter-culture had many manifestations, with its use of marijuana and psychedelic drugs like LSD, its sexual experiments, its rock festivals and 'happenings', its interest in Zen Buddhism and other forms of eastern mysticism, its communes and 'flower children'. Thousands of young people poured into the Haight-Ashbury district of San Francisco during the 'Summer of Love' of 1967; the area was soon known as Hashbury. Many younger Americans – and a few older – were trying to create alternative lifestyles, 'liberated', experimental and communal, which they fashioned as determined cultural assaults on conventional bourgeois values and lingering puritanical codes. For many respectable Americans, the 'hippies' came to stand as affronts both to American culture and to the American political order. It may be that the counter-culture enhanced the appeal of the New Left for some young Americans. On the other hand the counter-culture was not unproblematic for the New Left. It threatened to siphon off the energies of some young people, while also courting the hostility towards the New Left of American workers and others who might otherwise have joined them in resisting American capitalism.

With the New Left and the counter-culture spinning off in all directions as the Sixties advanced, some 'movement' members strove for an element of unity. They called the National Conference for New Politics in Chicago in August 1967, one aim of which was to consider the establishment of a new political party and another was to attempt to restore co-operation between white and black militants. Some 200 groups despatched about 2000 delegates, though only about 400 were African Americans. 'We're going to liberate you whether you want to be liberated or not', James Forman of SNCC told the delegates. Pacifist and liberal groups had participated in the call for the conference, but it was the minority of black radicals who dominated the proceedings, and they demanded 50 per cent of the conference votes. The white majority, whether out of guilt or empathy, meekly conceded these demands (which also ignored the claims of women). The New Left might unite in opposition to the Vietnam War, and the conference passed the usual anti-war resolutions, but the terrain of race was more difficult to negotiate. Todd Gitlin observed that 'They forced down whitey's throat the plain truth that the movement's momentum is mainly black'. The idea of a new party was dropped and the New Left was not provided with a clear political direction, though it had become evident that if white and black were to work together, it would be on black terms. The deference towards non-whites paralleled the growing iden- tification of many radicals with Third World revolutionaries. Minorities in the United States, in the context of global capitalism, could be seen as part of the colonized oppressed for whom figures like Che Guevara and Ho Chi Minh spoke.

As the New Left groups became more radical they also tended to fragment. And just as co-operation between radical and moderate activists became more difficult, so did that between black and white. As noted previously, as groups like SNCC and CORE developed black nationalist philosophies they cast off their white allies (and lost some of their funds). The second half of the 1960s witnessed the emergence of some very radical and indeed revolutionary groups, but schisms also abounded, and the New Left ultimately lost what little coherence it had been able to muster.

One issue on which the radical groups could sometimes make common cause was Vietnam. The anti-war movement was an amor- phous affair, very much larger than the New Left itself. It embraced veteran pacifists and socialists, students who were not drawn to other causes, artists and intellectuals like the poet Robert Lowell, and liberal senators like Eugene McCarthy. As the war escalated so did the oppo- sition. Martin Luther King's stand against the war in 1967 represented the defection from the president's side of a central strand of the civil rights movement. Moderates of largely middle-class organisations like SANE (National Committee for a Sane Nuclear Policy) and Women Strike for Peace mingled with clergymen, nuns, hippies and black mili- tants in anti-war demonstrations. The bulk of those who were members of the dozens of anti-war organisations were probably middle-class whites. The anti-war movement, it has been said, was 'more assembled than it was organized'.

The campuses had been a fertile breeding ground of the anti-war cause, and when deferments for students after their first four years of college was ended in the summer of 1967 opposition grew yet more. The draft had fallen particularly on the poorer classes, because the middle class youths at college could often secure more-or-less indefinite deferment, with many of them on graduation moving on to advanced professional courses. No group had been hit harder than blacks. African Americans constituted a disproportionately large component of combat troops. But from 1967 the middle classes had their idealism sharpened by a personal interest in questioning the validity of the war. Peace demonstrations were now supplemented by anti-draft protests, and induction centres were occasionally attacked. 'Hell no, we won't go!' became the cry.

The year 1967 was punctuated by large peace protests. There was a great peace march in New York in April, after which New Leftists organised the National Mobilisation Committee to End the War in Vietnam (known as Mobe). The Mobe organised a high profile demonstration in Washington in October, to conclude Stop the Draft Week, which was attended by such notables as Norman Mailer and Robert Lowell and some 100,000 other Americans. Blacks and whites joined together in this exercise, which culminated in a march on the Pentagon. The administration was so worried that 2,500 troops were posted inside the Pentagon and another 2,500 outside. The occasion was attended by some brutal scenes, as demonstrators were beaten with gun butts and 7,000 were arrested, and also by some surrealistic ones, as Abbie Hoffman led a motley crowd in an attempt to levitate the Pentagon. If the demonstration apparently did nothing to change government policy in Vietnam, it served momentarily to bring New Left and pacifist groups together.

By early 1968 the burning of draft cards had almost become a commonplace. The celebrated 'baby doctor' Dr Benjamin Spock was arrested for conspiring with others to break the draft law, his trial elevating him as the symbolic protector of the generation that his instruction manual had helped to raise. Two Catholic priests, Fathers Philip and Daniel Berrigan, achieved celebrity in orchestrating campaigns to destroy draft cards, to which end they invaded Selective Service offices. In June another priest broke into a draft office in Chicago and burned 20,000 files. The Berrigan brothers went to prison, although Dr Spock's conviction was overturned on appeal. But protests were becoming more violent. By the spring of 1968 ROTC (Reserve Officers' Training Corps) offices and other campus buildings were occasionally being burned or bombed. A few committed pacifists expressed their agonised beliefs by burning themselves to death.

The Mobe had decided after its march on the Pentagon to mount a major anti-war demonstration at the Democratic National Convention in 1968. Allied to the Mobe was the newly-formed Youth International Party, or the Yippies, led by Abbie Hoffman, who announced their own Festival of Life at Chicago. The New Left, in this incarnation largely identified with the SDS, and the Yippies, duly arrived in the city, perhaps 30,000 of them, and staged their protests. Long since warned of trouble, and fearing a riot of the kind which had torn apart other cities over the last few summers, Mayor Richard Daley had let it be known that his police would 'shoot to kill' arsonists and 'shoot to maim' looters. Denied permits to hold rallies, demonstrators were clubbed by the police in bloody scenes that displaced coverage of the convention on national television. The Yippies nonetheless succeeded in nominating a live pig called Pigasus for president.

The anti-war movement's impact is virtually impossible to gauge, although it has been credited with driving Lyndon Johnson from the White House. It may also have contributed to the election of Richard Nixon. By March 1968, according to a Gallup Poll, the proportion of Americans who believed that the United States should never have got involved in Vietnam reached a new high of 49 per cent. But that was in the aftermath of the Tet offensive, which did more to sap public confidence in US policy than the anti-war demonstrations themselves. Further, while the anti-war protests kept up the pressure and helped to force many in public life and the media to reconsider their attitude towards the war, they also provoked a backlash. Many Americans came to favour disengagement from Vietnam because they saw the war as a waste of men and money, a perception induced in part by New Left activity, but opinion polls also showed an overwhelming public disapproval of street protesters. In 1970 in New York angry building workers in their 'hard hats' physically assaulted anti-war demonstrators.

The resurgence of the anti-war movement during the Nixon administration underlined its detachment from the New Left, which was in the process of disintegrating. The New Left had been disenchanted by conventional politics for some years, as illustrated by the militancy of the black radicals and the periodic campus violence. That disenchantment was deepened further by the traumas of 1968, notably by the assassinations of Martin Luther King and Robert Kennedy, the scenes at

Chicago, and Nixon's triumph in November. It is hardly surprising that some elements, albeit small, were turning to thoughts of revolution and the use of force. How else could 'the system' be overthrown? One answer was the counter-culture. There were those who hoped to transform American society by transforming the consciousness of a great many Americans, thus leading them to a new enlightenment, even if by the use of drugs. But others contemplated less peaceable means.

At the beginning of the decade the SDS had seen universities as potential crucibles of radical reform, but before its end saw them as repressive symbols of the establishment, as instruments for maintaining a regimented society and for servicing the war machine. As the New Left moved further left, so universities became targets for direct action. One of the greatest confrontations occurred in April 1968 at Columbia, where the SDS was already engaged in disputes with the administration, notably over the university's military research contracts with the Pentagon. But the spark in April was the university's decision to build a gymnasium in a public park that had been frequented by blacks from neighbouring Harlem. Since earlier university expansion had already meant acquiring buildings previously tenanted by blacks and Puerto Ricans, this further invasion of their territory could be represented as a species of arrogant bureaucratic racism. Black student radicals and the mainly white SDS seized a number of campus buildings, ransacked the office of the president, and held three university officials 'hostage' for twenty-four hours. The occupiers refused to leave the buildings until granted amnesty, which was refused, and were finally forcibly removed by the police. The SDS claimed a victory, and the university did abandon the gym and gave up many of its defence contracts. But the 'Siege of Morningside Heights' also served as a model for other campus protests across the country. Over the next few years hundreds of campuses experienced occupations, though such activities hardly endeared students to the public at large. And the number of student radicals remained a minority. (A 1969 poll indicated that about 13 per cent of college students saw themselves as New Left, although that was substantially larger than the leftist sympathy in the population at large – among the same age group outside college a tiny 3 per cent identified with the New Left.)

But as its chapters were experimenting with the use of force, the SDS itself was being torn apart. The Progressive Labor (PL) group was trying to refashion it along Marxist lines, emphasising party discipline, revolution and a worker-student alliance. At the SDS national convention in June 1968 pictures of Stalin and Trotsky hung from the walls. But Marx, Lenin and even Mao were beginning to look a little old-fashioned when compared to such new heroes as Che Guevara and Ho Chi Minh, and those trying to stop a PL takeover sought to outflank it from the left, developing a strategy that became known as the Revolutionary Youth Movement in which the black radicals would serve as the vanguard of revolution. Yet another tendency was represented by a New York anarchist group named Up Against the Wall, Motherfuckers, or more simply, the Motherfuckers, and another by the San Francisco Bay Area Revolutionary Union. The struggles within SDS came to a head in 1969, by which time the national council had committed itself to 'the need for armed struggle as the only road to revolution'. The extreme radicals brandished the banner of 'support for the Vietnamese people, led by the National Liberation Front, and of all oppressed people in their struggle against imperialism'. They saw themselves as freedom fighters, empathising with Third World guerrillas in the struggle against the imperial enemy.

This route took the SDS out of the campuses, which had been their multiple base, and into the streets. At the annual convention in June the PL won control and the supporters of the Revolutionary Youth Movement broke away. The RYM itself quickly fragmented, with RYM II poised against the even more radical Weathermen. The Weathermen (or Weatherpeople, as some preferred) were soon trying to organise collectives in major cities with a view to fashioning revolutionary cells, and invading high schools and colleges in the (mainly vain) hope of winning recruits. In October they staged their celebrated Days of Rage in Chicago as the Chicago Eight were being tried. Some 300 turned up, and they dynamited a statue, smashed windows and cars, and most were arrested. In 1970 the surviving Weathermen went underground, from whence they plotted revolution and periodically bombed banks. The SDS, the group that came closest to providing a focus for the New Left, had collapsed.

Probably only a very few of those young Americans who had identified with the New Left sympathised with the Weathermen. Some clove to the host of other organisations that had participated in protest activity, such as CORE, the PL party, the Motherfuckers, and the Yippies (who also suffered from a form of schismatic disruption with the emergence of the Crazies, not to mention the Zippies). Black nationalist and revolutionary groups were also disrupted by internal dissension and police repression. Anti-war activity diminished with the phasing out of the draft in the early 1970s. But the scattered groups of the left, espousing contrasting ideologies and often suffering from declining memberships and funding, could hardly make common cause. Many New Leftists abandoned any pretence at political action and retreated to rural communes to get stoned and party with their friends. 'There were a lot of good, righteous people showing up in places like Vermont and New Hampshire in those days', recalled a former SDS president: '. . . I remember it with great fondness. It was almost the best part of the struggle. The best part of the struggle was the surrender'.

If the major political elements of the New Left were being eviscerated, the counter-culture still offered an escape. For some harassed radicals, perhaps, smoking dope, listening to rock music and the permissive life-styles of the hippies allowed them to express their dissatisfaction with American society without taking to the streets. Many lived together in communes or 'families', most famously in New York's East Village and in the Haight-Ashbury district of San Francisco, but also fairly liberally scattered across the United States. Rather as black nationalists searched for ways of creating separate institutions, so the counter-culture tried to build alternative communities. Where the militants flirted with or even occasionally engaged in violence, members of the counter-culture expressed themselves in 'love-ins' or in such festivals as 'Gentle Thursday', periodic celebrations of love and play staged for a few years by students at Austin in Texas. But for many participants the counter-culture was an instrument of change. They hoped that through spreading their cultural values and changing the consciousness of their fellow citizens, a structural transformation of society could in turn be effected. By the early 1970s some former political activists were joining new religious groups, whether in Zen centres, in ashrams, or as disciples of Eastern gurus. 'There is a race going on between religion and revolution to capture people's minds', observed Tom Hayden, 'and I'm afraid we're losing to the occult'.

The greatest counter-cultural happening of the decade was the Woodstock Festival, held in August 1969 in Bethel, New York. Extra-ordinary numbers showed up for this event, an estimated 400,000 over three days, dedicated to showing that love and co-operation represented a better way than making war in Vietnam. Joan Baez, Jimi Hendrix, and the Jefferson Airplane were among those who entertained the mighty crowds. But, like political activism, the counter-culture had its dark side too. Another festival was held in December at the Altamont Speedway in Livermore, California, when the Rolling Stones hired a group of Hell's Angels to keep order. But security was poor, and in the commotion one person was fatally stabbed by an Angel and one was apparently trampled to death. (According to Hell's Angel leader Sonny Barger, Keith Richards threatened that the band would stop playing unless the Angels cooled it: 'I stood next to him and stuck my pistol in his side and told him to start playing his guitar or he was dead. He played like a motherfucker.') Similarly unhelpful to the image of the counter-culture in 1969 were the murders in Los Angeles of the film actress Sharon Tate and six others by members of 'the family', as the commune led by Charles Manson was known. Manson, it seemed, disliked rich 'pigs'.

Yet the counter-culture did not collapse, at least not exactly, although entrepreneurial impulses both inside and outside it meant that significant aspects assumed an increasingly commercialised form. It never became a threat to the capitalist economy or established political institutions. But counter-cultural attitudes, conduct and artistic expressions gradually spread through a large part of American – and world – society. Drug use, long hair and rock music were hardly the exclusive preserve of the student generation. In 1970 Charles Reich in *The Greening of America* hailed the advent of Consciousness III, in which openness, spontaneity and feeling were displacing the rationality associated with the corporate order of Consciousness II. If Reich's vision of personal liberation was grossly optimistic, at least some Sixties' values were becoming more widespread by the Seventies. By 1973 the proportion of Americans who believed pre-marital sex was wrong had dropped to only one in two – it had been nearly four in five in 1959. By that date too about two-thirds of Americans were expressing tolerance of socialists and atheists, a much higher proportion than had earlier obtained. Joseph Veroff and his colleagues, in comparing questionnaire surveys undertaken in 1957 and 1976, found that Americans generally had become more interested in finding warmth and satisfaction in personal relationships. Humanistic psychology, it seems, had become the norm.

Perhaps no cause better reflected the survival of the spirit of the Sixties than feminism. When the organisations of the New Left were racked by disillusionment and subjected to fierce political and financial pressure, their female members could turn their energies to women's liberation. The women's movement suffered from its own divisions, but it was one of the triumphs of Sixties ferment, and it became an all but irresistible force in the 1970s.

Like civil rights, the women's movement did not come out of nowhere. The National Women's Party had existed since 1916 and was still lobbying Congress, and 'social feminists' – trade unionists and others – had long been working to improve conditions for working women. The latter's influence in the Democratic party had helped to persuade John Kennedy to appoint a Presidential Commission on the Status of Women in 1961. The number of working women had been growing, aided by the restructuring of the economy which provided more service and white (or pink) collar jobs, and by 1960 over 38 per cent of women were going out to work. The traditional notion that a woman's place was with her family was being called into question.

Yet the active members of the National Women's Party were elderly and few in number, while the President's Commission proved cautious in approach, calling for equal pay for women but also for special training for young women for marriage and motherhood. The implication was that women were still mothers first and workers second. It declined to support the Equal Rights Amendment, an old feminist cause designed to give both sexes identical constitutional rights, fearing that this would jeopardise the protective legislation for women that had been so arduously built up. The President's Commission represented liberals who hoped to work with government rather than radicals prepared to challenge it. The call for equal pay was formally met in 1963, and a surprise victory was won in 1964 with an amendment to the Civil Rights Act banning discrimination on grounds of sex as well as of race, religion and national origin. Nonetheless, these were rather hollow victories, for the Equal Employment Opportunity Commission (set up to enforce the Civil Rights Act) showed little interest in upholding women's rights, and some women – like some black activists – began to lose patience with trying to work with the administration.

When Betty Friedan's book, *The Feminine Mystique*, was published in 1963 the time was ripe for it, and it quickly became a best-seller. The 'feminine mystique' that Friedan assaulted was the 1950s' ideology placing women in the home. The suburban, middle-class women that Friedan studied had conformed to the feminine mystique, trying to fulfil themselves as wives and mothers but experiencing instead a profound unhappiness. Their homes had become 'comfortable concentration camps' in which they lived empty, unrewarding lives. Women, said

Friedan, had been denied the means to develop their talents as individual human beings. Men had the opportunities to find out what they were good at, to test their talents and ambitions, but the feminine mystique had allowed women roles only as housewives and mothers, and their individuality had been stunted.

In many ways there was nothing new in what Friedan said, and her passionate polemic exaggerated and distorted women's plight. Its focus on middle-class college women, for example, slighted the experiences of working-class and minority women, few of whom were trapped in 'comfortable concentration camps'. But the book touched a responsive chord. Friedan clearly articulated what many women were feeling. Her book was a success in part because the traditional ideology was out-of-synch with the times. Had the feminine mystique been as pervasive as she suggested, had women generally and passively accepted their prescribed role, it is difficult to see how the book could have sold so well. But women had not been performing their traditional role for nearly a generation. There were more women at work than ever before, many of them wives and mothers. The book was particularly popular with young college women. In some respects Friedan was echoing what the SDS had been saying about the stultifying nature of material affluence, although in her case she was inviting her readers to look to their own interests rather than those of others.

In the affluent society of the 1960s there were many jobs for women to take – as typists, teachers, nurses, sales assistants and the like. But many college-educated women aspired to more than this, seeing no reason why they should not pursue much the same careers as their boyfriends. Thoughts of this sort fuelled the emerging women's movement. In 1966 Betty Friedan and others founded the National Organization for Women (NOW), which demanded 'a fully equal partnership of the sexes, as part of the worldwide revolution of human rights'. NOW soon committed itself to two main causes, the Equal Rights Amendment and 'the right of women to control their reproductive lives', which meant abortion. The ERA had been a feminist demand since the 1920s, but suddenly young activists in the Sixties were seizing the cause. Abortion too was a radical demand and it disturbed many otherwise sympathetic women. The Women's Equity Action League, led by professional and academic women, broke away in 1968 to concentrate on economic and legal action. But abortion had a powerful appeal to many young and educated women who wanted to remove any obstacles to their right to climb as high as their talents would take them, and NOW expanded in membership. As more young and radical women joined it, NOW moved to the left and became more confrontational in its methods. The modern feminist movement was erupting, its demand for equal rights putting it on a trajectory that would lead it into collisions with other powerful forces.

Rights philosophies can divide movements, and more radical feminist groups were soon splintering off. Many of the women participating in these had been active in the civil rights and New Left movements, where they had encountered the philosophy of participatory democracy, with its insistence that individuals should have a say in those decisions that affected their lives, and where they were daily prompted to contemplate the meaning of equal rights. Yet such ideals were not always observed in these movements. Many black women in SNCC, for example, came to resent the domestic and secretarial roles that they were often assigned, and white women experienced something similar in the SDS. For the most part, black women tended nonetheless to accept that civil rights demanded their first loyalty, but increasingly young white women were tempted to break away. The anti-war movement could grate on female sensibilities too, as when draft-resisters used the slogan 'Girls say yes to boys who say no'. Many young women came to recognise the need to separate the cause of women's rights from that of any other movement. As one put it: 'We intend to make our own analysis of the system, and put our interests first, whether or not it is convenient for the Left'.

By 1967 groups of dissatisfied women were meeting to explore their needs, and as consciousness-raising sessions took off they were led into discussions of the degree to which women were the subjects of male repression. The personal was becoming the political. Women could be seen as the victims of 'sexism', a new term, much as African Americans were the victims of racism. In September 1968 such women staged a dramatic protest at Atlantic City during the Miss America Pageant, scorning its degrading symbolism and crowning a live sheep Miss America. A more sophisticated explication of this philosophy was published in 1970 in the form of Kate Millett's *Sexual Politics*, which argued that sexism was a product of a patriarchal system that structured the whole society. An implication of this approach was that the policy changes and constitutional amendments favoured by NOW would be woefully insufficient to effect the liberation of women. To Shulamith

Firestone, NOW was 'more a leftover of the old feminism rather than a model of the new'. Where black radicals could have no faith in a power structure commanded by whites, radical feminists had no hope in one commanded by men. For the liberationists, capitalism and patriarchy themselves had to be overthrown.

Such revolutionary currents spawned an array of new groups. In 1968 a radical faction split away from NOW to become The Feminists. In 1969 such groups as the Redstockings and the Radicalesbians appeared, and several others too in such cosmopolitan centres as New York and San Francisco. Spurred by their more radical sisters, even the professional women of NOW became more militant, participating in demonstrations, abortion speak-outs and other forms of direct action. They co-operated with other groups in pressing for abortion reform, which meant persuading state legislatures to change the law, and by about 1970 such states as New York and California were agreeing to abortion on demand. In 1973 the Supreme Court handed down its historic decision in *Roe v. Wade*, upholding a woman's right to terminate pregnancy and prohibiting states from banning early abortions.

At the same time as the abortion cause was gaining success, however, other issues were dividing the women's movement. One radical strand to emerge in the late 1960s had insisted that men were the enemy, and that heterosexual relationships themselves were oppressive. This kind of logic led the Radicalesbians to the position that only lesbianism was politically correct. When Kate Millett proclaimed her lesbianism in December 1970, NOW was racked by controversy. Betty Friedan, still wanting to lead women into the mainstream, feared that NOW's primary objectives would be swept away in a popular backlash if it became identified with the lesbian cause, but others sympathised with Millett's stand. NOW was seriously disrupted, but the broader feminist cause continued its bold advance. The magazine *Ms* began publication in 1972 and many women were soon claiming the new form of address. Women's studies proliferated in colleges, and a network of women's groups, centres, and publications spread out across the land. Women were creating their own communities.

If the women's movement drew on the civil rights movement, it in turn encouraged some men to become more conscious of their rights. If women wanted control over their own bodies and held that the personal was political, homosexuals could argue much the same. In June 1969 a police raid on a gay bar in New York's Greenwich Village precipitated a riot as gay men fought back, the troubles rumbling on for a week and culminating in a protest march. The 'Stonewall Riots' gained wide publicity and helped to precipitate the formation of the Gay Liberation Front. A year later some 5000 gays and lesbians proudly marched to celebrate the anniversary of Stonewall.

The decade that had begun with a demand for black equality at a Greensboro lunch-counter ended with the slogan 'Gay Power' scrawled on the buildings of Greenwich Village. Liberation politics touched Americans of many kinds. Native Americans, Mexican Americans, and Puerto Ricans articulated their own nationalist philosophies. Before long other ethnic groups like Irish Americans and Polish Americans were stirred to assert their identity. In 1970 over 50,000 Italian Americans gathered in New York to demand 'Italian Power'. In the 1970s too such movements as Grey Power and children's rights emerged. The protests of the Sixties had served to make Americans more conscious of their rights, and the claim to rights had been extended from individuals to groups. Affirmative action programmes represented an official endorsement of the concept of group entitlements.

At the beginning of the Sixties much of the media had projected images of American society in which white middle class (and male) values were assumed to be the norm. If the unspoken premise was that the United States was still a kind of melting pot in which the different ingredients would eventually merge into a homogeneous whole, in an identity dominated by an Anglo-Saxon heritage, such premises could not easily have survived the experiences of the decade. In fact, like the political consensus that had depended on turning a blind eye to the condition of southern blacks, the cultural consensus of the 1950s had been largely a contrivance, a product in part of a Cold War quest for security and of a media projecting itself to a suburban audience. The protest movements of the 1960s tore this image apart, exposing the fracture lines of race, ethnicity, gender, class and occupation. And insofar as minorities had previously sought assimilation in a consensual order, the liberation currents of the Sixties inspired them to change direction and to cherish their distinctive identities and assert their rights.

The pursuit of rights created a politics of pluralism of unwonted pervasiveness. This is not to suggest that the white middle classes had abandoned their commitment to the primacy of their values, as they showed in the election and re-election of Richard Nixon to the presidency. But the United States had become a land marked more by variety than homogeneity. Political polarisation was paralleled by cultural fragmentation, and American society resembled a mosaic of living pieces. Each cultural fragment, however, offered the individuals adhering to it a sense of community in an era of disconcerting change.

Conclusion

The optimism and activism of the Sixties did not die with the decade but they weakened. So many of the hopes of the Sixties – the abolition of poverty, the elimination of racial discrimination, the elevation of the Third World – had not been fulfilled. It became more difficult to enlist in a cause with any confidence. The number of applications to the Peace Corps began to drop from 1967 and never regained the buoyancy of the mid-1960s; in 1976 the figure was less than half that for 1966. There were fewer allies for progressive reform in government and in the courts and therefore less point in pressing a cause, as the prospect for revolution also seemed even fainter than ever. In any case, many liberals and radicals came to share with conservatives some scepticism as to whether government could successfully discharge the responsi-bilities that had been heaped upon it. It was more difficult to see the nation state as a progressive force. Little wonder that some activists turned to drugs or religion (or both) in the 1970s, either in a quest for personal salvation or in the hope that a transformed consciousness could be transmitted to the larger society. Many got on with their lives as best they could, often becoming teachers, lawyers, social workers, doctors, academics, or journalists, that is engaging in occupations in which they could continue to cherish the values they had embraced in the Sixties.

The heritage of the Sixties was a mixed one. The discovery that the United States lacked both the economic strength and the military might to impose its will on a recalcitrant world was a humbling one, but the new awareness of limits at least encouraged a questioning of America's Cold War mission. The Sixties bequeathed a richer and more varied cultural life and more tolerant moral attitudes, although these counter-cultural traits were to coexist uneasily with a shriller assertion of identity politics. Poverty was reduced and rights dramatically extended, but in the quarter century following Richard Nixon's re-election the wealth of the economic elite grew while the real earnings of ordinary workers did not. The suspicion of authority arising from the Sixties encouraged the greater scrutiny of public figures by the press and the strengthening of the mechanisms of accountability, but at the cost of a reversion to a system of government in which sustained policy-making was difficult.

The contradictions inherent in the New Deal Order were exposed by the demands of the Sixties, and the hegemony of the Democratic party was over. With the break-up of the New Deal coalition went the credibility of American liberalism, undone by an arrogant foreign policy and by domestic programmes that could not bear all the hopes invested in them. But if the electorate lost confidence in liberal reform, it displayed little enthusiasm for the political alternatives. The agenda of right-wing Republicanism had been decisively defeated in 1964, and when American voters later put a more moderate Richard Nixon into the White House they also maintained Democratic majorities in Congress. The prescriptions of the New Left, of course, appealed to only a tiny minority, and the futile turn of the Weathermen to violence was symbolised by the self-destruction of some of their members when their bomb-making equipment exploded at their town house in Greenwich Village in 1970. If liberalism had lost its way, so had radicalism, and while the anti-New Left conservatism of Richard Nixon prepared the ground for the rise of the New Right, its triumph was never to be complete. Even the popular Ronald Reagan was to encounter Democratic majorities in both houses of Congress during most of his presidency.

The electorate's revival of the system of checks and balances reflected a renewed distrust of politicians and government. The electorate itself was tending to diminish as a proportion of American population, and becoming increasingly middle class in composition. But the retreat from conventional politics may also have reflected, at least in small part, a greater determination on the part of many to take control of their own lives, itself a Sixties aspiration. The efforts by counter-cultural activists to fashion their own communities were paralleled by the extraordinary attempts by African Americans, women, gays, ethnic and other cultural groups to build their own networks and institutions. These could function as an alternative to traditional party politics, and at local level many Americans were able to create supportive community structures, as they also sometimes established lobbying institutions to bring their interests to bear on the various levels of government.

The sharper awareness both of rights and of group identities continued to inform movements of many kinds. Rights are not easily compromised, and the public arena became characterised by endless contest. But it was also recognised that the public too had rights. The movements of the Sixties had demanded more from government while preaching a distrust of both government and business; 'public interest' groups were the natural outcome. A strong public interest movement emerged to monitor and criticise the performance of the regulatory and other public agencies. It pressed for the more effective disciplining of business behaviour, particularly through securing a greater recognition of the concept of public rights by the courts. The class actions by consumers against the tobacco industry at the end of the twentieth century could be regarded as one long-term consequence of 1960s activism.

Whatever the weaknesses of the post-industrial theorists, they had glimpsed something of the future. They had usually assumed an enhanced role for central government, and the retreat from 'big government' ideas did not arrest the erosion of the autonomy of local authorities by a resilient federal bureaucracy and by agencies and courts anxious to extend national standards. The 'knowledge society' and information technology seemed even more in evidence by the end of the century than had been the case when sociologists were pointing to their emergence in the 1960s. Such theorists had appreciated too that the changing social structure would create new constituencies, inject new issues, and alter the shape of the political landscape. Corporate America remained powerful, but the kind of class conflict that had helped to shape the New Deal, with its orientation towards labour, was being overshadowed by other configurations. The pursuit and protection of economic interest remained a central feature of a capitalist order, but had to be accommodated to demands rooted in lifestyle, culture, gender, and ethnicity. The environmental movement, for example, was largely promoted by middle-class professional activists, recruited from the expanded white-collar class that was to a degree insulated from the profit motive. It could be seen as an expression of the social ethic that some theorists had believed would become stronger in a post-industrial society.

The Sixties were not in vain. White and male America had surrendered some of its authority. If women and members of racial minorities continued to find obstacles to their progress, at least they were admitted to the competitive race for fortune and a few of them succeeded. President Clinton was pleased to appoint a cabinet that 'looked like America', where Anglo-Saxon males were joined by women, African Americans, Hispanics, and Jews. But the progress achieved by some was not shared by all. As the number of women in the higher professions rose sharply, a literature emerged pointing to the simultaneous 'feminisation' of poverty. Broadly, the proportion of poor Americans declined in the aftermath of the Great Society, but the per centage of the poor that was female edged up. This phenomenon was the product of a number of complex social processes, among them a growth in the number of female-headed households (which in turn was a reflection of the greater variety of family structures associated with the post-industrial order). In other words, women's experience was a bifurcated one: some prospered and others did not. Much the same was true of African Americans and Hispanics, as a few joined the highest social and economic ranks and others remained trapped in urban ghettos or rural poverty. In a sense, this divided experience was a mark of the successful integration of women and ethnic groups into the larger capitalist economy, even if the number of those who reached the highest positions fell far short of their proportions of the population. In the last third of the twentieth century economic stratification was tending to increase; the distance between rich and poor Americans generally was growing.

The dismantling of the formal racial and gender barriers in the Sixties made it easier to appreciate the heterogeneous nature of American society. Awareness of cultural differences had been heightened, and Americans of many kinds became more sensitive to their ethnic and cultural identities, as some became more aggressive in their claims. The rediscovery of ethnicity also encouraged a greater variety of lifestyles and artistic expression, as did the seductive counter-culture of the Sixties. Only a few joined communes, but Americans experimented with more diversified forms of family structure as they also cautiously adjusted to more 'permissive' conduct. Public opinion polls in the 1970s suggested that Americans were becoming more tolerant of racial, religious, and political differences, even if conservative values remained strong among those who cast votes. Larger numbers of Americans claimed to find fulfilment in personal relationships. For many, it seemed, the pursuit of happiness was becoming an individual and private quest. But the Sixties' emphasis on personal autonomy could take many forms and contributed to the heightened consciousness of rights. Perhaps one unhappy legacy of the Sixties was the ferocious explosion in lawsuits that characterised the closing decades of the twentieth century.

Suggestions for Further Reading

While a decade may constitute only ten years, the Sixties were marked by such momentous episodes that an enormous literature has been generated. Such topics as the Great Society, the New Left, the civil rights movement and the Vietnam War have each inspired extensive literatures of their own, and this brief guide is necessarily highly selective.

One introduction to the Sixties is by way of books which encompass longer periods. Among the best general studies of the post-war United States are William H. Chafe, *The Unfinished Journey: America since World War II* (New York: 3rd edn., Oxford University Press, 1995), James T. Patterson, *Grand Expectations: the United States, 1945–1974* (New York: Oxford University Press, 1996), and James Gilbert, *Another Chance: Postwar America, 1945–1968* (New York: Knopf, 1981). In examining the decade itself, historians have tended to divide between those who emphasise the disintegration of American society and politics and those who stress the constructive and liberating aspects. The former view tends to prevail among the slightly older but still valuable studies of the decade. Allen J. Matusow, *The Unraveling of America: a History of Liberalism in the 1960s* (New York: Harper & Row, 1984), broadcasts his message in his title and takes issue with the inadequacy of liberal programmes. William L. O'Neill, *Coming Apart: An Informal History of America in the 1960's* (Chicago: Quadrangle Books, 1971), also dwells on the process of fragmentation, and Godfrey Hodgson, *America in Our Time* (New York: Vintage Books, 1978), examines the emergence and subsequent decline of the 'liberal consensus' among the governing classes. Good on political history but from a similar perspective is John M. Blum, *Years of Discord: American Politics and Society 1961–1974* (New York: Norton, 1991). Discord and dissolution also loom large in a number of lively recent studies. David

Steigerwald, *The Sixties and the End of Modern America* (New York: St Martin's Press, 1995), sees the decade as one in which the orderly values of 'modernist' liberalism were displaced by 'postmodernist' dislocation, ambiguity and mutability; David Burner, *Making Peace with the 60s* (Princeton: Princeton University Press, 1996) emphasises the destructive effects of the splitting apart of liberalism and radicalism; Maurice Isserman and Michael Kazin, *America Divided: the Civil War of the 1960's* (New York: Oxford University Press, 1999) skilfully balances the customary focus on the political left with proper attention to the right. Sympathetic treatments which discern some change for the better include David Chalmers, *And the Crooked Places Made Straight: The Struggle for Social Change in the 1960s* (Baltimore: Johns Hopkins University Press, 1991), which places the upheavals of the decade in the context of an often liberating transformation of consciousness, and David Farber, *The Age of Great Dreams: America in the 1960s* (New York: Hill & Wang, 1994), which found that a consumer-oriented society in the grip of fundamental change emerged both more egalitarian and more polarised.

Students will also find useful several of the volumes in Heath's Major Problems series (Lexington, MA: D. C. Heath), which include both contemporary documents and important essays by modern scholars. Among them are Robert Griffith, ed., *Major Problems in American History Since 1945* (1992); Robert J. McMahon, ed., *Major Problems in the History of the Vietnam War* (1995); and Mary Beth Norton and Ruth M. Alexander, eds., *Major Problems in American Women's History* (1996). Some of the more suggestive analyses of the decade and of particular episodes within it are to be found in collections of essays, most notably Robert H. Bremner, Gary W. Reichard and Richard J. Hopkins, eds. *American Choices: Social Dilemmas and Public Policy since 1960* (Columbus: Ohio State University Press, 1986); Barbara L. Tischler, ed., *Sights on the Sixties* (New Brunswick: Rutgers University Press, 1992), which includes Ellen Herman's, 'Being and Doing'; David Farber, ed., *The Sixties: From Memory to History* (Chapel Hill: University of North Carolina Press, 1994); Brian Balogh, ed., *Integrating the Sixties* (University Park: Pennsylvania State University Press, 1996); and Stephen Macedo, *Reassessing the Sixties: Debating the Political and Cultural Legacy* (New York: Norton, 1997). For essays and readings of from a radical perspective see Sohna Sayres et al., *The 60s Without Apology* (Minneapolis: University of Minnesota Press, 1984), which includes Fredric Jameson's essay on 'Periodizing the 60s'. Steve Fraser and Gary Gerstle, eds., *The Rise and Fall of the New Deal Order, 1930–1980* (Princeton: Princeton University Press, 1989) is invaluable on the transformation of the political system.

Studies of topics peculiarly associated with the spirit of the Sixties include Gerard T. Rice, *The Bold Experiment: JFK's Peace Corps* (Notre Dame: University Notre Dame Press, 1985); Elizabeth Cobbs Hoffman, *All You Need Is Love: The Peace Corps and the Spirit of the 1960s* (Cambridge, MA: Harvard University Press, 1998); and Walter A. McDougall, *The Heavens and the Earth: A Political History of the Space Age* (New York: Basic Books, 1985). The activism of the Supreme Court was also distinctive; see, for example, Arthur J. Goldberg, *Equal Justice: The Warren Era of the Supreme Court* (Evanston: Northwestern University Press, 1971) and Morton J. Horwitz, *The Warren Court and the Pursuit of Justice: A Critical Issue* (New York: Hill & Wang, 1998).

The United States, of course, was not the only society to be rocked by the currents of the Sixties. A rare attempt to take a comparative view is Arthur Marwick, *The Sixties: Cultural Revolution in Britain, France, Italy, and the United States, c.1958–c.1974* (Oxford: Oxford University Press, 1998), which dismisses interpretations that stress fragmentation and destruction. David Caute, *1968: The Year of the Barricades* (London: Hamish Hamilton, 1988) explores the international dimensions of a momentous year. Paul Berman, *A Tale of Two Utopias: The Political Journey of the Generation of 1968* (New York: Norton, 1996) also attempts a global perspective on what he sees as the self-destructive rebel groups of the 1960s.

Post-industrial theory is classically expressed by Daniel Bell in *The Coming of Post-Industrial Society* (New York: Basic Books, 1973); see too his *The Cultural Contradictions of Capitalism* (London: 2nd edn., Heinemann, 1979). Also suggestive, though critical of the Bell formulation, is Scott Lash and John Urry, *The End of Organized Capitalism* (Cambridge: Polity Press, 1987). Useful for social and economic change are William Issel, *Social Change in the United States, 1945–1983* (Basingstoke: Macmillan, 1985) and Michael French, *US Economic History since 1945* (Manchester: Manchester University Press, 1997). An insightful analysis of economic policy is David P. Calleo, *The Imperious Economy* (Cambridge, MA: Harvard University Press, 1982); see also, Seymour E. Harris, *The Economics of the Political Parties: with Special Attention to Presidents Eisenhower and Kennedy* (New York: Macmillan, 1962), and

Wallace C. Peterson, *Silent Depression: the Fate of the American Dream* (New York: Norton, 1994). Important specialised studies include Herbert Stein, *The Fiscal Revolution in America* (Chicago: University of Chicago Press, 1969) and Kim McQuaid, *Uneasy Partners: Big Business in American Politics, 1945–1990* (Baltimore: Johns Hopkins University Press, 1994). Studies on major aspects of social history include Kenneth Jackson, *Crabgrass Frontier: The Suburbanization of the United States* (New York: Oxford University Press, 1985); Elaine Tyler May, *Homeward Bound: American Families in the Cold War Era* (New York: Basic Books, 1988); and Robert Wuthnow, *The Restructuring of American Religion: Society and Faith since World War II* (Princeton: Princeton University Press, 1988). Indispensable for tracing the course of public opinion is George Gallup, *The Gallup Poll: Public Opinion, 1935–1971* (Westport: Greenwood Press, 1972).

Good studies of long-term political change include Iwan W. Morgan, *Beyond the Liberal Consensus: A Political History of the United States since 1965* (London: Hurst & Co., 1994), and, with a political science perspective, Everett Carll Ladd with Charles D. Hadley, *Transformation of the American Party System: Political Coalitions from the New Deal to the 1970s* (New York: Norton, 1978). Textbooks by political scientists are often useful for understanding parties and politics, such as Tim Hames and Nicol Rae, *Governing America: History, Culture, Institutions, Organisation, Policy* (Manchester: Manchester University Press, 1996) and David McKay, *American Politics & Society* (Oxford: 3rd edn, Blackwell, 1993). Interesting analyses may be found in Byron E. Shafer et al., *Present Discontents: American Politics in the Very Late Twentieth Century* (Chatham, NJ: Chatham House Publishers, 1997). Still useful on elections are Theodore H. White, *The Making of the President, 1960* (London: Cape, 1962) and the subsequent studies of *1964* (London: Cape, 1965) and *1968* (New York: Atheneum, 1969). Particular aspects of the politics of the Sixties are examined in James L. Sundquist, *Politics and Policy: The Eisenhower, Kennedy and Johnson Years* (Washington: Brookings Institution, 1968) and Gareth Davies, *From Opportunity to Entitlement: The Transformation and Decline of Great Society Liberalism* (Lawrence: University Press of Kansas, 1996).

In national politics the turbulence of the Sixties tended to facilitate the revival of conservatism. On this subject see Thomas Byrne Edsall with Mary D. Edsall, *Chain Reaction: the Impact of Race, Rights and Taxes on American Politics* (New York: Norton, 1992); Mary C. Brennan, *Turning*

Right in the Sixties: The Conservative Capture of the GOP (Chapel Hill: University of North Carolina Press, 1995); and William C. Berman, *America's Right Turn: From Nixon to Bush* (Baltimore: Johns Hopkins University Press, 1994). Major studies of conservative figures include Robert Alan Goldberg, *Barry Goldwater* (New Haven: Yale University Press, 1995) and Dan T. Carter, *The Politics of Rage: George Wallace, the Origins of the New Conservatism, and the Transformation of American Politics* (New York: Simon & Schuster, 1995).

There are several studies of the various presidential administrations. Two members of the Kennedy White House early provided accounts for a president who could not write his own memoirs: Arthur M. Schlesinger Jr, *A Thousand Days: John F. Kennedy in the White House* (Boston: Houghton Mifflin, 1965) and Theodore C. Sorensen, *Kennedy* (London: Hodder, 1965). Good scholarly studies include Herbert S. Parmet, *JFK: The Presidency of John F. Kennedy* (New York: Dial Press, 1983); James N. Giglio, *The Presidency of John F. Kennedy* (Lawrence: University Press of Kansas, 1991); and Hugh Brogan's sympathetic and witty, *Kennedy* (London: Longman, 1996.) A favourable treatment is Irving Bernstein, *Promises Kept: John F. Kennedy's New Frontier* (New York: Oxford University Press, 1991) and a hostile one is Thomas C. Reeves, *A Question of Character: A Life of John F. Kennedy* (New York: Free Press, 1991). Lyndon Johnson was able to provide his own account in *The Vantage Point: Perspectives of the Presidency, 1963–1969* (New York: Holt, Rinehart and Winston, 1971), though much more revealing is Doris Kearns, *Lyndon Johnson and the American Dream* (New York: Harper & Row, 1976), written after extensive interviews with the former president. Concise and judicious is Paul Conkin, *Big Daddy from the Pedernales: Lyndon Johnson* (Boston: Twayne, 1986), while the most authoritative scholarly account is Robert Dallek, *Flawed Giant: Lyndon Johnson and His Times, 1961–1973* (New York: Oxford University Press, 1998). Containing some useful insights is Rowland Evans & Robert Novak, *Lyndon Johnson: The Exercise of Power* (New York: New American Library, 1966). Richard Nixon was also able to tell his own story in *RN: The Memoirs of Richard Nixon* (London: Sidgwick & Jackson, 1978), and, despite blistering analyses of his role in Watergate, he has received surprisingly sympathetic treatment by at least some biographers, as in Herbert S. Parmet, *Richard Nixon and His America* (Boston: Little, Brown, 1990) and Melvin Small, *The Presidency of Richard Nixon* (Lawrence: University Press of Kansas, 1999).

The social policies of Sixties administrations have given rise to extensive literature. The anti-poverty programmes may be approached through Daniel Knapp & Kenneth Polk, *Scouting the War on Poverty: Social Reform Politics in the Kennedy Administration* (Lexington: Heath, 1971), James T. Patterson, *America's Struggle against Poverty, 1900–1985* (Cambridge, MA: Harvard University Press, 1986), and Edward D. Berkowitz, *America's Welfare State: from Roosevelt to Reagan* (Baltimore: Johns Hopkins University Press, 1991). Charles A. Murray, *Losing Ground: American Social Policy, 1950–1980* (New York: Basic Books, 1984) criticises Great Society programmes for creating dependency, while John E. Schwarz, *America's Hidden Success: a Reassessment of Twenty Years of Public Policy* (New York: Norton, 1984) argues that they helped to reduce poverty. Fascinating on the Great Society's engagement with the race issue is Nicholas Lemann, *The Promised Land: The Great Black Migration and How It Changed America* (London: Macmillan, 1991). Educational policies are examined in Diane Ravitch, *The Troubled Crusade: American Education, 1945–1980* (New York: Basic Books, 1983) and Hugh Davis Graham, *The Uncertain Triumph: Federal Education Policy in the Kennedy and Johnson Years* (Chapel Hill: University of North Carolina Press, 1984). On environmental issues see Samuel P. Hays, *Beauty, Health and Permanence: Environmental Politics in the United States, 1955–1985* (Cambridge: Cambridge University Press, 1987), and Kirkpatrick Sale, *The Green Revolution: The Environmental Movement, 1962–1992* (New York: Hill & Wang, 1993).

Stephen E. Ambrose, *Rise to Globalism: American Foreign Policy, 1938–1970* (Harmondsworth: Penguin, 1971) is a useful introduction to foreign policy issues. Thomas G. Paterson offers some sharp analyses in *Meeting the Communist Threat: Truman to Reagan* (New York: Oxford University Press, 1988). Generally critical of Kennedy are the essays in Thomas G. Paterson, ed., *Kennedy's Quest for Victory: American Foreign Policy, 1961–1963* (New York: Oxford University Press, 1989). A recent brief introduction to Vietnam is Mitchell K. Hall, *The Vietnam War* (Harlow: Longman, 2000); see also John Dumbrell, *Vietnam: American Involvement at Home and Abroad* (British Association for American Studies, 1992) and Michael H. Hunt, *Lyndon Johnson's War: America's Cold War Crusade in Vietnam, 1945–1968* (New York: Hill & Wang, 1996). Substantial, authoritative accounts include George Herring, *America's Longest War: The United States and Vietnam, 1950–1975* (Philadelphia: 2nd edn., Temple University Press, 1986); Marilyn

Young, *The Vietnam Wars: 1945–1990* (New York: HarperCollins, 1991); and Stanley Karnow, *Vietnam: A History* (New York: Viking, 1983). Absorbing on the American war leadership is David Halberstam, *The Best and the Brightest* (London: Barrie & Jenkins, 1972). Focusing on the Johnson White House is Larry Berman, *Lyndon Johnson's War: The Road to Stalemate in Vietnam* (New York: Norton, 1989) and Herbert Y. Schandler, *The Unmaking of a President: Lyndon Johnson and Vietnam* (Princeton: Princeton University Press, 1977). For the domestic implications of the war see Thomas Powers, *The War at Home: Vietnam and the American People, 1964–1968* (New York: Grossman, 1973) and Tom Wells, *The War Within: America's Battle over Vietnam* (Berkeley: University of California Press, 1994). An interesting recent analysis of the anti-war movement is Rhodri Jeffreys-Jones, *Peace Now: American Society and the Ending of the Vietnam War* (New Haven: Yale University Press, 1999). On the anti-war movement's impact see Melvin Small, *Johnson, Nixon, and the Doves* (New Brunswick: Rutgers University Press, 1988).

As with Vietnam, space allows mention of only the tip of the iceberg of literature on civil rights. C. Vann Woodward's seminal *The Strange Career of Jim Crow* (New York: 3rd edn., Oxford University Press, 1974) remains an absorbing starting point. Good modern introductions include Robert Cook, *Sweet Land of Liberty? The African-American Struggle for Civil Rights in the 20th Century* (London: Longman, 1998) and William M. T. Riches, *The Civil Rights Movement* (London: Macmillan, 1997). Other valuable general studies include Manning Marable, *Race, Reform and Rebellion: the Second Reconstruction in Black America, 1945–1982* (London: Macmillan, 1984); Harvard Sitkoff, *The Struggle for Black Equality, 1954–1980* (New York: Hill & Wang, 1981); and Robert Weisbrot, *Freedom Bound: A History of America's Civil Rights Movement* (New York: Norton, 1990). For King's role see Adam Fairclough, *To Redeem the Soul of America: The Southern Christian Leadership Conference and Martin Luther King Jr.*, (Athens: University of Georgia Press, 1987); David Garrow, *Bearing the Cross: Martin Luther King Jr., and the Southern Christian Leadership Conference, 1955–1968* (New York: Morrow, 1986); and the two volumes by Taylor Branch: *Parting the Waters: America in the King Years, 1954–63* (London: Macmillan, 1988) and *Pillar of Fire: America in the King Years, 1963–1965* (New York: Simon & Schuster, 1998). Important specialised studies include Doug McAdam, *Political Process and the Development of Black Insurgency, 1930–1970* (Chicago: University of Chicago Press, 1983); Aldon D. Morris, *The Origins of the Civil Rights Movement: Black Communities Organizing for Change* (New York: Free Press, 1984); August Meier & Elliott Rudwick, *CORE: A Study of the Civil Rights Movement* (New York: Oxford University Press, 1973); and Clayborne Carson, *In Struggle: SNCC and the Black Awakening of the 1960s* (Cambridge, MA: Harvard University Press, 1981). Good on the intellectual history, showing how the movement's quest for freedom encouraged self-transformation, is Richard H. King, *Civil Rights and the Idea of Freedom* (Athens: University of Georgia Press, 1996). Valuable for understanding the evolution of race relations in the South are Steven F. Lawson's two volumes, *Black Ballots: Voting Rights in the South, 1944–1969* (New York: Columbia University Press, 1976) and *In Pursuit of Power: Southern Blacks and Electoral Politics, 1965–1982* (New York: Columbia University Press, 1985), and also David R. Goldfield, *Black, White, and Southern: Race Relations and Southern Culture, 1940 to the Present* (Baton Rouge: Louisiana State University Press, 1990). Brian Ward, *Just My Soul Responding: Rhythm and Blues, Black Consciousness and Race Relations* (London: UCL Press, 1998) expertly illuminates the interrelationship between music and African American politics. On the emergence of Black Power see Stokely Carmichael & Charles V. Hamilton, *Black Power: The Politics of Liberation in America* (New York: Vintage, 1967); Philip S. Foner, ed., *The Black Panthers Speak* (Philadelphia: Lippincott, 1970); and William L. Van Deburg, *New Day in Babylon: The Black Power Movement and American Culture, 1965–1975* (Chicago: University of Chicago Press, 1992).

The turmoil of the decade has received due attention. Putting violence in perspective as well as amassing much information is Hugh Davis Graham & Ted Robert Gurr, eds., *The History of Violence in America: Historical and Comparative Perspectives* (New York: Bantam, 1969); see also the Kerner Commission's *Report of the National Advisory Commission on Civil Disorders* (New York: Bantam, 1968) and James W. Button, *Black Violence: Political Impact of the 1960s Riots* (Princeton: Princeton University Press, 1978).

Essential reading on the New Left is the participatory history by Todd Gitlin, *The Sixties: Years of Hope, Days of Rage* (New York: Bantam, 1989). See also James Miller, *Democracy is in the Streets: from Port Huron to the Siege of Chicago* (New York: Simon & Schuster, 1987); Wini Breines, *Community and Organization in the New Left, 1962–1968:*

The Great Refusal (New York: Praeger, 1982); and Peter B. Levy, *The New Left and Labor in the 1960s* (Urbana: University of Illinois Press, 1994). A major study of protest activity is Terry H. Anderson, *The Movement and the Sixties* (New York: Oxford University Press, 1996). A critical confrontation is addressed in David Farber, *Chicago '68* (Chicago: University of Chicago Press, 1988). For a hostile critique of the New Left see Peter Collier & David Horowitz, *Destructive Generation: Second Thoughts About the '60s* (New York: Summit Books, 1989). Theodore Roszak defined the counter-culture in *The Making of a Counter Culture: Reflections on the Technocratic Society and its Youthful Opposition* (London: Faber, 1970); for a sociological analysis see J. Milton Yinger, *Countercultures: The Promise and Peril of a World Turned Upside Down* (New York: Free Press, 1982). George McKay, *Senseless Acts of Beauty: Cultures of Resistance since the Sixties* (London: Verso, 1996), while focused more on Britain than the United States, argues that modern lifestyle politics rewrites the 1960s 'minus the politics'.

A useful introduction to women's history is Carl N. Degler, *At Odds: Women and the Family in America from the Revolution to the Present* (New York: Oxford University Press, 1980), as is Rosalind Rosenberg, *Divided Lives: American Women in the Twentieth Century* (New York: Hill & Wang, 1992). Betty Friedan, *The Feminine Mystique* (New York: Norton, 1963), helped to inspire the feminist revival, and her role is examined in Daniel Horowitz, *Betty Friedan and the Making of The Feminine Mystique* (Amherst: University of Massachusetts Press, 1998). Important on the origins and character of the modern movement is Sara Evans, *Personal Politics: The Roots of Women's Liberation in the Civil Rights Movement and the New Left* (New York: Knopf, 1979). See also Cynthia Harrison, *On Account of Sex: The Politics of Women's Issues 1945–1968* (Berkeley: University of California Press, 1988). Gay liberation is discussed in John D'Emilio and Estelle B. Freedman, *Intimate Matters: A History of Sexuality in America* (Chicago: 2nd edn., University of Chicago Press, 1997).

Index